THE AHMADIS

THE AHMADIS

Community, Gender, and Politics in a Muslim Society

ANTONIO GUALTIERI

McGill-Queen's University Press
Montreal & Kingston • London • Ithaca

To our grandsons, NICOLA and ZACHARIE, the next generation

© McGill-Queen's University Press 2004
ISBN 0-7735-2737-0 (cloth)
ISBN 0-7735-2738-9 (paper)

Legal deposit third quarter 2004
Bibliothèque nationale du Québec

Printed in Canada on acid-free paper that is 100% ancient forest free (100% post-consumer recycled), processed chlorine free

McGill-Queen's University Press acknowledges the support of the Canada Council for the Arts for our publishing program. We also acknowledge the financial support of the Government of Canada through the Book Publishing Industry Development Program (BPIDP) for our publishing activities.

NATIONAL LIBRARY OF CANADA CATALOGUING IN PUBLICATION

Gualtieri, Antonio R., 1931–
The Ahmadis: community, gender, and politics in a Muslim society / Antonio Gualtieri.
Includes bibliographical references and index.
ISBN 0-7735-2737-0
ISBN 0-7735-2738-9
1. Ahmadiyya members – Pakistan.   2. Ahmadiyya.   3. Pakistan – Politics and government.   4. Persecution – Pakistan.   I. Title.
BP195.A5G818 2004   297'.86'095491   C2004-900991-5

Typeset in 10.5/14 Adobe Caslon with Meta+ and Linotype Pide Nashe One display. Book design and typesetting by zijn digital.

CONTENTS

INTRODUCTION
Tradition and Modernity

This book builds on work I did in 1987, some of which was published as *Conscience and Coercion: Ahmadi Muslims and Orthodoxy in Pakistan.* To my surprise that book garnered a modest reputation for me as an expert on Ahmadiyyat, which only proves that in the land of the blind the one-eyed man is king. I was frequently called by the Refugee Board of Canada to advise on immigration questions about Ahmadis and was invited to lecture in Montreal mainly to Refugee Board judges on "The Persecution of Ahmadi Muslims in Pakistan and Their Status as Refugees in Canada." I was told by the organizer that *Conscience and Coercion* had become their bible in adjudicating Ahmadi refugee claimants from Pakistan.

The question I address in the present book is the Ahmadi handling of the tension between tradition and modernity. The Ahmadis present a provocative instance of this general concern. They are a highly conservative community in doctrine, ritual observance, and moral obedience, and, at the same time, a highly educated group with universal literacy and a large number of professionals, which implicates them in the modern naturalistic ethos characterized by reliance on science and technology. They have built the biggest mosque in North America at Maple, north of Toronto – an achievement that suggests the community's ease of functioning within Canada's economic and professional life.

The Ahmadis hold uncompromisingly to a conservative theology that relies on a supernatural level of being, divine intervention, and the promulgation of a divine law culminating in a last judgment in which the righteous will be received by God's mercy into everlasting paradise. This theology stresses supernatural prophetic revelation in the divine disclosures pre-eminently to the Prophet Muhammad in Arabia in the seventh century AD and latterly to Mirza Ghulam Ahmad of Qadian (in the present-day Indian Punjab) towards the end of the nineteenth century. Their way of life is correspondingly strict, grounded as it is in a divinely prescribed pattern that entails, among other things, parental authority, close family life, a disposition towards gender-specific roles, and separation of the sexes.

The point at which the debate between tradition and modernity crystallizes most challengingly is the question of gender relations. My main concern is how the gender issue illuminates the broader concern of what happens when a traditional revelatory world view and value system comes into collision with the individual ethos of modernity that asserts the rights of men or women to pursue a way of life that meets their own desires, private value systems, and inclinations, so long as it does not do any palpable external harm to anyone else.

The problem was thrown into relief soon after our arrival in Rabwah in 1995 when Monsoor Khan, director of foreign missions for the Ahmadi movement, visited us in our bungalow. Monsoor told us that when he was a missionary in Britain, two girls of his Ahmadi flock, perhaps sixteen and eighteen, did a very uncharacteristic thing by running away from home because they could no longer tolerate their parents' control or the imposition of what they experienced as an inflexible regime. The fear was that they would run off with boyfriends, a prospect that seemed to terrify the Ahmadi community more than anything else. They called upon the police for help and the officer with whom Monsoor spoke said, "I sympathize with your concerns, I share them myself; however you must understand that we cannot do anything as the girls are of an age where they are free to make these decisions." Monsoor said that he was vexed to the depth of his soul for ten days and could scarcely sleep or eat until he got some word as to the girls' whereabouts.

This anecdote exemplified the conflict that provides the theoretical framework of my research. On the one hand, there is the traditional perspective, world view, and value system of the Ahmadis with their emphasis on community, the *umma*, the faithful people who are committed to the divine revelation in the Qur'an to which they add their obedience to the Promised Messiah.

Against that stands the perspective of modernity, which is characterized by a liberal democratic ethos that stresses individual rights. The Ahmadis felt that they were obliged to emphasize and prize the girls' participation in and loyalty to their community, pre-eminently to their families. The British justice system, on the other hand, asserted the individual rights of the girls. As it turned out, the story had a happy ending: after ten days the girls disclosed their whereabouts and indicated that while they were not cohabiting with boyfriends, they were determined to remain apart from their parents with whom they felt they had reached an irreconcilable impasse. Among other things, the episode shows how the different social and political perspectives of the two world views can generate practical pastoral concerns among the missionaries and the religious community.

To stress the nature of the problem, I suggested that Monsoor and the Ahmadi leadership would have to confront the changing way of life as Ahmadi Muslim women move from the security and insularity of Rabwah to Toronto or Calgary. Even now some Ahmadi women with professional educations have moved into the workforce where they consort with men who are neither their husbands nor their fathers nor their brothers. It is likely that many more will be inclined to do so in the future. This raises serious concerns about the propriety of gender mixing relative to some Muslim demands for female modesty and segregation. I asked Monsoor whether this might lead to two levels of Islamic fidelity for Muslim women. Would the women of Rabwah be regarded as better Muslims than those of Toronto because the women in Rabwah walk the streets not only in black burqa – an ankle-length garment resembling a long loose raincoat – with head covering but also with black veils across the lower face? The women in Toronto, though well covered in the traditional Punjabi *shalwar kameez* – baggy trousers and a long knee-length shirt – might have only a flimsy head scarf over their hair, leaving their faces exposed. They project a feminine image that in Rabwah is hidden away under the loose black coverings worn by the women. Might they thus be considered to be less in conformity with Qur'anic requirements than the women in Rabwah? Monsoor recognized that this is a problem that may require a hardening of the lines as to what is required of women if they are to live in fidelity to shari'a; alternatively it may imply a reinterpretation of purdah that gives women greater freedom in dress and behaviour while still allowing them to remain obedient to the Islamic values of feminine modesty and becomingness in the face of male physical demands upon women. The authority of shari'a remains paramount since this is God's holy law whose main sources lie in the Qur'an and Hadith – those traditions that relate the customary conduct of the Prophet Muhammad. These are some of the issues that will have to be faced.

What is the connection between modernity and the abandonment of traditional gender roles? If we take as the hallmark of modernity Weber's concept of rationalization in *The Protestant Ethic and the Spirit of Capitalism*, the nature of the connection comes within our purview. Rationalization entails the methodical organization of human life and activity in the most efficient manner possible for economic gain – profit and ever more profit. Rationalized economic efficiency requires interchangeable units of productivity. It reduces people to abstract entities on the analogy of the machine. Just as the machine has no feelings, emotional ties, or communicative solidarities, the human as an extension of a machine partakes of those same qualities of abstraction and impersonality. To strip human productive agents of as many aspects of their particularity as possible is to work in the direction of economic efficiency.

One of the particularities that might be seen to interfere with rationalized economic activity is that of gender, distinct sexual natures, and gender roles. If men and women are considered ontologically to be adapted in gender-specific ways to the accomplishment of certain roles, they will be recalcitrant to an impersonal mechanistic productive process. Thus, from the point of view of economic rationalization, gender specificity is a liability and should be eliminated. By analogy the collectivities of family and clan that are so central to the social organization of traditional societies also come to be viewed as impediments to economic rationalization. This became clear in the early days of industrialization when the productive locus moved from the cottage and the hearth to specialized factories.

From the point of view of modern economic rationalization, traditional culture's emphasis on family and clan is irrational given that production tends to be subordinated to the maintenance of these human loyalties and obligations. A case in point may be the extensive hospitality that was shown us during our stay in Lahore. We were escorted around by some highly trained professionals who took whole days off work to show us their city – all in fulfillment of the traditional Islamic conception of hospitality to the guest. Giving expression in this way to the obligation and privilege of serving the guest is hardly congenial to economic production and gain, but it is the manifestation of a different value system that subordinates economic rationalization to the economically irrational goals of social connectedness and adhering to communal affections and loyalties. Likewise, it may not be economically productive to encourage women to forego remuneration in order to pursue the domestic role of child bearer, nurturer, and homemaker but it does reveal fidelity to a competing set of values that runs counter to the impetus of modernity to expunge the personal, including the social connections and solidarities that are the defining traits of people in traditional societies.

To help with my research, our daughter, a PhD in Middle Eastern history, conducted preliminary interviews with fifteen Ahmadi women in Toronto, some working in the public sphere and others engaged in the more typical domestic role. Subsequently, my wife, Peggy, accompanied me on our trip to Pakistan in 1995; otherwise I would have had no access to women's perceptions. In four previous trips to Pakistan I never saw the mothers, wives, or postpubescent daughters of the households in which I stayed. At the *jalsas*, or national annual meetings, that we have attended in Canada, the women (who are present in equal numbers with the men) are accommodated in separate marquees and follow the proceedings on closed-circuit television. At banquets in modern hotels that in some ways epitomize the Western style, the women dine in separate halls or partitioned areas.

Gender issues did not exhaust my enquiry. In my interviews I sought to absorb and analyze whatever would serve as clues to an Ahmadi perspective on the conflict between a traditional world view and value system and a modern one. This entailed investigation into the organization of Ahmadi communal life, including its ritual dimension, and the Ahmadi response to the harassment and persecution they endure at the hands of orthodox mullahs and the government criminal justice system.

I discussed my research proposal with the late Khalifatul Masih IV, head of the community, who in 1984 had fled to London from Pakistan, where his life was in peril. Because the Ahmadis are, in many ways, a strongly hierarchical and authoritarian body, no research can be undertaken without his approval. Hazoor (to use his affectionate honorific) gave cordial endorsement to my research. Needless to say, he placed absolutely no constraints on the intellectual product of my investigation, just as he had never asked to see the manuscript of *Conscience and Coercion* before its publication, trusting that it would be as accurate and fair as it was within my scholarly capacity to make it.

We proceeded to Pakistan to the spiritual centre and headquarters at Rabwah where the Ahmadi Missionary Training College is located (the Ahmadis conduct a vigorous missionary outreach, one of the reasons they incur the displeasure of Sunni theologians). Also at Rabwah are their internal court, principal cemeteries, and certain administrative offices such as the directorates of education and foreign affairs. The status of Rabwah in Ahmadi piety and regulation is somewhat ambiguous. The pilgrimage destinations of Mecca and Medinah remain, of course, the geographical focal point for all Muslims, including Ahmadis. The most distinctive sacred site for the Ahmadis is still Qadian in the Indian Punjab, where the Promised Messiah received his revelations and where he is buried. Administratively, moreover, while Rabwah is important, the focus must be where the khalifa resides, for he bears the ongoing authority of the Promised Messiah (for which reason he is called khalifa, or deputy; see Appendix 2) and is the conduit of divine guidance and grace in the present. Rabwah occupies a middle ground between Qadian and London, the khalifa's temporary headquarters. After the partition of the Indian subcontinent in 1947, the Ahmadi khalifa arranged for a Pakistani military escort to accompany all the Ahmadis who had taken shelter in Qadian along with numerous other Muslims who had gravitated there as a haven. A large segment of the Ahmadi community relocated to Rabwah, which remained the governing centre of the movement until the khalifa's departure. Three hundred and thirteen Ahmadis were left behind in Qadian to care for the religious sites, chief of which, of course, is the cemetery and the burial place of the Promised Messiah. The Ahmadi remnant in India have been cut off from the Ahmadi community in Pakistan and abroad and have become fossilized. Their attitudes are those of fifty years ago at the time of partition. A friend of ours, Dr Latif Qureshi, characterized them as being like Sufis. When one recalls, however, that one of the formative influences on Mirza Ghulam Ahmed was Sufi thought, it may be that the Ahmadis of Qadian have retained some of the piety that prevailed in the last part of the nineteenth century and shaped the outlook of the founder. Rabwah meanwhile still emanates an Ahmadi ethos because of its preponderant Ahmadi population.

We lived in Rabwah for three months conducting interviews not only with the principal leadership of Ahmadiyyat but also with returned and retired missionaries and other functionaries and members. We also visited (and revisited) some of the *jama'ats* (congregations) dispersed throughout Pakistan. My goal was to understand the existential orientations, attitudes, values, conflicts, and aspirations of Ahmadis especially as they relate to the friction between the Ahmadis' Islamic tradition and their encounter with modernity, and then to describe this Ahmadi life experience faithfully and accurately to my readers.

The terrorist attacks on the World Trade Center in New York and the Pentagon on 11 September 2001 and the subsequent Anglo-American bombing of Afghanistan have given this study a timeliness that we could not have imagined when it was undertaken. In earlier years the Ahmadi leadership had warned that if the international community remained unconcerned with the persecution of Ahmadis by fanatical Muslim fundamentalists in Pakistan, it might subsequently find this same exclusivist and absolutist fanaticism rebounding on its own head. How prescient that admonition turned out to be. The same Manichaean hatred that targeted the Ahmadis for apostasy has now been directed towards the West – particularly the United States and modern American culture – as the enemy of Islam.

These events, manifesting Islam's ongoing struggle to deal with – by way of rejection or accommodation – the modern world may give this study a relevance and usefulness beyond what I had hoped.

We were picked up by Idris at the Dar al Zikar Ahmadi mosque in Lahore and made our departure for the old city before noon. Idris, amir of the Lahore district, is the brother of Hamid Khan, amir of the Lahore *jama'at*, and nephew of Zafrulla Khan (1893–1985), probably the best-known Ahmadi apart from the khalifas themselves. Zafrulla Khan was the first foreign minister of Pakistan after the formation of the state in 1947. Then he was elected President of the General Assembly. Later he was a judge with the International Court of Justice in The Hague and Pakistan's ambassador to the United Nations in New York.

Lahore was jammed with the usual cars, scooters, motor rickshaws, carts, donkeys, bicycles, camels, and jostling pedestrians in a way that makes me wonder how we ever managed in 1972–73 when we drove our Volkswagen van with our four young children from England across Asia and down into southern India. I can only assume that the traffic then was somewhat lighter than it is now, although my recollection is that it was congested and impenetrable. It was a luxury not to have to rely upon public transportation and I think that at our age we are entitled to this freedom of movement. In any case we certainly relish it.

Idris took us west towards the old city by a different route than any we had previously followed through very busy commercial areas – commercial in the sense of harbouring a multitude of shops. The closer we got to the old city the more congested the traffic became. Heavily-laden trucks carried materials from factories and warehouses to the shops. The area through which we passed was largely wholesale, crowded with enormous stacks of aluminum pots, glass, pottery, car-repair parts, bicycles, bicycle parts, etc.

As we got closer to the old walled city Idris picked up Shaikh Rahmat Ali, an older but still vigorous wiry man who was to be our guide through the lanes and *gullis* (narrow passageways), from which the English word gully is derived. Idris reported that Rahmat, his simple Punjabi clothing notwithstanding, was a multimillionaire in Pakistani rupee terms. His money was made in the cloth industry. Later we visited his shop where he presented Peggy with an exquisite shawl.

On another clear late January morning, Peggy and I went with our lawyer friend Ijaz from Dar-al-Zikar to the Shalimar Mughal Gardens on the east outskirts of Lahore. Much of the original marble facing on the walls of the garden enclosure and the arcades and pavilions had been stripped by the Sikhs during their almost-hundred-year hegemony in the Punjab after they had defeated the Mughals and before the British in turn defeated them.

The gardens were used as an encampment by the Mughals in their yearly procession from the winter residence in Delhi to their summer camp in Srinigar in the Vale of Kashmir. Their route took them westward from Delhi to Lahore and then northward through Sialkot over the Banial Pass and then down into the Kashmir valley.

The most striking thing about the Shalimar Gardens was the hordes of schoolchildren – some of them very smart in their white *shalwar kameez* with navy blue blazers and coloured scarves, or *dupatta*. They seemed as a group extraordinarily happy and buoyant. Many of them called out in English, "Good morning, How are you, Where are you from?" Others importuned us to pose with them for photos taken on their own cameras. Some schoolgirls were not wearing uniforms but only their customary colourful *shalwar kameez*; we presumed they were from state schools. We were struck by the exuberance of these young children and especially some of the young girls, who were verging on puberty but showed no signs of the stereotypical Muslim reserve, instead smiling boldly at us and calling out to Peggy and me.

One morning at 5:20 a.m. I set off for the Ahmadi mosque of Dar-al-Zikar (House of Worship) just as the call to prayer (*azhan*) began to sound from loudspeakers at a local Sunni mosque. The Ahmadis are forbidden by law to give the *azhan* on the grounds that in doing so they would be feigning to be Muslims and subjected to a three-year imprisonment. Similarly, the government prohibits the Ahmadi use of loudspeakers, a characteristic part of all mosque activity in Pakistan. I am quite certain that the loudspeaker was designed to be an irritant to the Ahmadis because the towers upon which it was set were in close proximity to the compound of the Ahmadi mosque and it blared at great volume. For the next fifteen minutes the call to prayer was echoed by surrounding mosques, but none of them matched in intensity the volume of the one set up close to the Ahmadi mosque.

I arrived just as the first Indonesian pilgrims began to enter the mosque. They stood near the blank walls in silent prayer and their numbers increased over the next fifteen minutes to twenty-seven or so when the prayers began. I sat in a chair against the back wall of the mosque and reflected that an observer of religions from outerspace might mistake the natural gas heater, with its red glow, for the central icon in the alcove (*mihrab*) that marks the *qibla*, or direction of prayer. In fact, there are no sacred icons within Islamic ritual save perhaps the geographical orientation itself.

After the formal prayer, the missionary who had served as imam for the prayers sat on the straw mats and discoursed with some of the participants, mainly the Indonesians and Malaysians. They viewed him as an authoritative teacher on Qur'an and Ahmadiyyat and were gleaning last words of instruction from him on this the morning of their departure for home.

THE AHMADIS

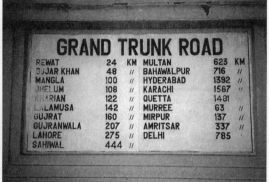

LEFT: In a tonga leaving the theological college where Nino had given a lecture

RIGHT: The author's research in Pakistan took him from the Karakoram's K2 in the north to Karachi in the south and from the Khyber Pass in the west to the Indian border east of Lahore

LEFT: Nino at the top of rock "mountain" with Rabwah below

RIGHT: Peggy with Ijaz Khan in the courtyard of the glorious Badshahi Mosque in Lahore

LEFT: Red sandstone walls inlaid with white marble in geometric patterns at the tomb of Jahangir in Lahore. The heavy wooden doors are hand-carved. Jahangir's tomb was built by his son Shah Jahan in 1627. In 1631 Shah Jahan's beloved wife, Mumtaz Muhal, died in childbirth. He supervised the building of her tomb, the Taj Mahal in Agra, India, constructed by 20,000 workers from 1623–43. One can see in Jahangir's tomb a portent of the glorious pietra dura which reached its height in the tombs of the Taj Mahal

RIGHT: Jahangir's tomb with decorative pietra dura

CHAPTER ONE

Setting the Scene

Defining Terms

In the course of my research I often encountered a gap between what I meant by such terms as modern, secular, science, natural, and supernatural and what the Ahmadis understood by those concepts. This was inevitable, and it may be useful to examine these divergent understandings since they bear directly on the tension between tradition and modernity.

Most of my Ahmadi interlocutors thought that to be modern is good. To be modern is progressive and rational, relying on intelligence and reflection on natural and human affairs. My use of "modern," on the other hand, reflects the Nietzschean legacy as something that is wooden, mediocre, flat, impoverished, and detrimental to the imaginative and mythic dimension of human consciousness. Modernity as a naturalistic and materialistic ethos is the challenge that a traditional society has to confront.

For my purposes, modernity implies (1) a worldview and a compatible value system that stresses an exclusive reliance on empirical scientific method for knowledge and excludes traditional reliance on another level of knowledge deriving from prophetic revelation or mystic trance; (2) a reliance on human technical mastery in the solution of all problems rather than the traditional invocation of supernatural agencies to deal with problems from sickness to drought to lost luggage; and (3) an emphasis on a this-worldly destiny that repudiates traditional affirmations of a supernatural teleology for human beings. The paradigm case for Protestantism might well be the Westminister catechism. To the question "What is the proper end of man?" the answer is given: "The proper end of man is to glorify God and enjoy him forever." Although modernity has produced the fax machine and heart/lung equipment, genetic engineering and in vitro fertilization, atom bombs and global pollution, this technical spectacle is not the defining feature of modernity as an ideology but rather those elements that I have adumbrated.

My use of the concept "secular" was fairly readily understood, although even here I have run into Ahmadi constructions that rehabilitate the term so that it has a positive significance to them. This becomes intelligible when one understands the social context out of which much of their analysis proceeds. Secular for them is the antithesis of the mullah-dominated theocracy that imposes prohibitions on freedom of religion in Pakistan. In order that we could be talking about the same things or at least using categories and concepts in a uniform way, I found that I usually had to rehearse the dimensions of secularism as I understand it, namely, a movement of consciousness and culture that emerges from the cognitive, technical, and teleological revolution of traditional world views and value systems. Secularism represents a reliance on scientifically derived knowledge and, as with modernity, the dismissal of revelatory claims for supernaturally initiated knowledge; it entails a reliance on human energy and intelligence in the resolution of problems rather than a reliance on supernatural helping agencies; and secularism presupposes that human purposes and ends have to be achieved within this space-time frame without appeal to another level of reality or supernatural destiny or afterlife. It entails not only this sort of metaphysical or ideological perspective but also certain social arrangements, such as functional differentiation, bureaucracy, and, somewhat paradoxically, liberal individualism and the erosion of the natural solidarities of kin, clan, and family that are so vital to traditionalist societies.

As for the terms natural and supernatural, I had thought that the Ahmadis would respond immediately with approbation to my appeal to supernatural revelation and supernatural intervention as the necessary corollary of their reliance on prayer for guidance and the solutions of problems. What I found, until the issue was clarified, was insistence that Ahmadi confidence in miraculous solutions to problems in response to prayer is entirely natural. This is a common confusion. The word "natural" can mean, in the first place, something that simply occurs – the natural is the self-evident, the existing. Natural can mean, in the second place, something that occurs spontaneously and unreflectively; in the third place, it can mean that which is inevitable and in conformity with unbreakable laws. I found it necessary to point out that in theological discourse, "natural" typically is a metaphysical term that signifies the reduction of all reality to a space-time frame of reference and the operation of things according to a uniform structure that is formulable as natural law. Against this background, supernatural then signifies an appeal to a level of being beyond the space-time dimension, a realm of reality, moreover, that can intervene within the space-time order to achieve ends that would not normally occur according to the intrinsic operation of natural law.

One night in Rabwah, we had dinner at the home of an army brigadier who was also a cardiologist. In the process of trying to elaborate the characteristics of modernity, I landed in a recurrent problem to do with divergent understandings of the concept of science. One of the animating impulses within secular modernity is the reliance on science that emerges from the seventeenth century onwards for both knowledge and problem solving. Scientific knowledge as the paradigm of all valid knowledge, and technology based on scientific grasp of the structures of the world, undergird the secular enterprise.

Most of my Ahmadi informants immediately rejoined that Islam in no way runs counter to science and they pointed to their own careers as confirmation. At this particular dinner, there were an engineer who operated a chipboard factory, a cardiologist with postgraduate qualifications from a Western university, and an opthamologist, also with advanced training in the West, who had attended General Zia-ul-Haq for eye problems.

They all insisted on the compatibility of Islam with science. I pointed out the distinction between science and scientism, conceding that there is no real problem in reconciling science with traditional confidence in revelation as the source of salvific knowledge. The problem emerges in the ideological superstructure that has been constructed on the basis of scientific method so that science becomes the exclusive avenue to any valid knowledge. One can be devoted to science without buying into the positivist scientistic ideology that excludes any appeal to sources of knowledge other than those available through scientific method.

The Ahmadis compared their position with that of their fundamentalist mullah opponents* who claim, for example, that it is impossible to land on the moon because of the intrinsic sanctity of the moon, which forbids such a project. The Ahmadis by contrast insist that science can never falsify faith. This is reminiscent, of course, for any who trained in Western philosophy and theology, of the Thomistic synthesis of nature and supernature. Thomas Aquinas held that grace does not destroy nature or the knowledge of nature but rather perfects it or completes it with the revelatory disclosure of things about God and salvation that would never be known apart from the special divine initiative in the gracious revelation in Jesus Christ. Natural knowledge, in turn, can never contradict the knowledge that comes through revelation. Natural theology and revealed theology exist in a harmonious synthesis in the Thomistic scheme. This resonates with the Muslim confidence in the compatibility of science and religion.

The controversy is not about science, however, but about a secular ideology that takes its point of departure from scientific knowledge but is not identical with it. I reminded my Ahmadi friends at dinner that their

---

* "The fundamentalist says there was a moment in history when a particular book, leader, or original social community was perfect. In their selective retrieval they try to go back to that perfect moment" (Marty, Appelby, *Fundamentalism Observed*). This is both true and untrue of the Ahmadis. As devout followers of Muhammad and adherents of the revealed book God sent down to him, they do harken back to the paradigmatic moment of divine disclosure in Arabia in the seventh century. At the same time their conception of ongoing revelation to the Promised Messiah and to his successor khalifas opens the door to new insight and divine guidance in subsequent eras.

unabashed collective reliance on prayer for the solution of problems is different from the secularist reliance on human rationality and technical power. There is a story of how Zafrulla Khan, in looking for one of his contact lenses and having vainly called upon his grandchildren for help, finally decided in desperation to raise the matter with God, imploring him, if he so willed, to help him find it. Whereupon his eye immediately caught a gleam of light that fell upon his contact lens, which had got caught up in some drapery. General Ali Malik, the Pakistani hero of the battle of Chowindah in 1965, had told me that his victory over superior Indian forces on the Kashmir front was due to God's response to his prayer. The two surgeons present at dinner testified to their reliance on prayer in the performance of their medical tasks. They were quite insistent that they just bind the wounds while God does the healing, and this in response to their persistent and earnest prayers. General Hassan, one of the surgeons present, also bore witness to his repeated experience of divine blessing upon generosity in the name of God. Anything that he gives in service of God returns to him the Qur'anic seven hundred times and more. This is clearly a world of meaning and experience that the secularist finds bizarre.

In trying to explain, especially to Mujeeb-ur-Rahman, the amir of the Rawalpindi *jama'at* who represented the Ahmadis in court against charges of "posing as a Muslim" or blasphemy (see chapter 6), who took the lead in this theological discussion, how it is possible for religious beliefs to be falsified by scientific findings, I gave the following examples. Some Christian conservatives have held that on biblical evidence the world was created in 4004 BC. This clearly contradicts the geological evidence that the world and human life are of much greater antiquity. How is the contradiction between science and revelation to be resolved? Some Christian conservatives opt for revelation and have recourse to such explanations as that God created the world in 4004 BC but implanted evidence of a much greater antiquity in order to test people's faith, to challenge them to believe God's revealed word rather than the deliverances of finite and fallible human reason. With this kind of thinking, religious beliefs can never be falsified, because no amount of evidence would ever be allowed to count against the revealed religious affirmation.

To cite another example, Christian revelation affirms the bodily resurrection of Jesus Christ. But if archaeologists and historians were to ascertain that a particular grave in Srinigar was indeed the tomb of Jesus, their scientific enterprise would invalidate the revealed claim of bodily resurrection and bodily ascension into heaven. (I chose this example deliberately to conform to the Ahmadi conviction that Jesus did not die on the cross and did not ascend bodily into heaven but, rather, once healed of his wounds from the cross, wandered to the East and died at the age of 120 in Kashmir where he was entombed.) Such contradictions confront Christians with two choices. One is to heed the deliverances of science and dismiss the revelatory beliefs as wrong, the products of ignorance or superstition, or as mythic expressions of spiritual and existential truths. The contrary position requires Christians to repudiate human scientific and rational evidence and heed only God's word in the revealed book. Mujeeb-ur-Raman's reply was that this problem emerges only because Christians have misunderstood their own revelation, particularly regarding the bodily assumption of Jesus into heaven, which the Ahmadis do not believe. Paradoxically, this is precisely the answer that most secularists give. In handling the conflict between scientific reason and revelatory belief they have decided that the belief is spurious, which is what Mujeeb asserted with respect to the particular Christian beliefs of Christ's resurrection and ascension. What he would not allow, of course, is that in the Islamic case there could ever be scientific evidence that would count decisively against a revealed fact or belief.

Our Ahmadi informants would have been hard pressed to appreciate the cultural dissonance (not to say hypocrisy) that V.S. Naipaul, in *Among the Believers* (page 158), vindictively ascribes to Maulana Mawdudi, "the patron saint of the Islamic fundamentalists in Pakistan" who "campaigned for Islamic laws without stating what those laws should be."

He died while I was in Pakistan. But he didn't die in Pakistan: the news of his death came from Boston. At the end of his long and cantankerous life the Maulana had gone against all his high principles. He had gone to a Boston hospital to look for health; he had at the very end entrusted himself to the skill and science of the civilization he had tried to shield his followers from. He had sought, as someone said to me (not all Pakistanis are fundamentalists) to reap where he had not wanted his people to sow. Of the Maulana it might be said that he had gone to his well-deserved place in heaven by way of Boston; and that he went at least part of the way by Boeing.

For Ahmadis, Islam, truly understood, is quite compatible with science and technology and there would be no contradiction in a devout Muslim seeking the benefits of medical science in Boston as well as Karachi.

The theme of the compatibility of science and the Qur'an was raised often enough to indicate that it is part of the Ahmadi ethos – a harmony so pronounced as to allow science to act as a confirmation of the truth of the Qur'an. This is redolent of an outmoded nineteenth-century liberal Protestant apologetics that in effect deferred to science, subscribing to an uncritical and extravagant view of science that justified its use to bolster revelational claims. Ahmadiyyat has not gone through the existentialist and cognitive crisis that characterized Christian thought in the post-WWII era and still seems comfortable with a rationalistic apologetics grounded in the capacity of science to confirm Qur'anic truth claims, thus serving to vindicate the authority of the Qur'an. What is not often discerned is the impact of this kind of defence both on the doctrine of God and on the doctrine of revelation.

One form that this scientific apologetic takes is to legitimate miracles by seeing them as the operation of natural laws as yet unapprehended by humans. Occurrences that seem so irregular and peculiar to us now but that are contained in the Qur'an or the Hadith of the Prophet will in the future be seen as events flowing from the divinely implanted regularities of nature, which in the present state of science are not yet known. The consequence of this line of thinking is to remove the miraculous from revelation, the spiritual life, and, in effect, the omnipotence of God. Once re-explained as phenomena that occur according to the operation of natural laws that are an innate (though not as yet understood) part of the natural realm, extraordinary events are no longer miraculous signs of the omnipotence and special purpose of God and thus vindications of his power, wisdom, and glory. Instead they are merely part of the intrinsic working of things. It seems not to be recognized that one consequence of this way of thinking is a devaluation of the omnipotence of God.

There is a curious and perhaps even contradictory cohabitation within Ahmadi mentality of a traditionalist piety of miraculous supernature alongside a confidence, even deference, towards the scientific enterprise and its rational explanations of events. A physicist who currently works as a top-level railway executive explained to me after a wedding at the *wallima* feast that the big bang theory of contemporary cosmology is anticipated in the Qur'an. Similarly, contemporary debates about whether the universe is infinitely expanding or will eventually collapse back on itself into some super-dense black hole is anticipated in the Qur'an, which opts for the contracting cosmology. I was also informed that present-day genetics is anticipated in the Qur'an. The intention of this line of argument is to validate the truth claims of the Qur'an by confirming them through scientific knowledge that we did not have until fourteen hundred years after the Qur'anic declarations.

The other consequence of this apologetic defence of the Qur'an is its impact on revelation. It comes very close to making one's confidence in the Qur'an as the revealed word of God dependent upon the confirmation of science. I pointed out how this worked to the detriment of Christian tradition in a past era when it was held that the Bible taught both that the first human was created as a single and complete act of God and that the world was created in 4004 BC, according to an interpretation of the chronology of Genesis. The conflict between these biblical views and the evolutionary findings of Darwin, whereby the human species evolves according to intrinsic laws of natural selection, and the discoveries of geology and palaeontology, which indicate that the world and the human species are far older than Genesis suggests, forced Christians of the late nineteenth century and on into the twentieth to choose between the authority of science and the authority of the Bible. Alternatively, Protestant apologetics pursued a kind of biblical winnowing that allowed people to affirm, on the one hand, the scientific truth of Darwin and, on the other, the truth of the claims for supernatural redemption made in the Bible. This was achieved generally by separating out a redemptive kernel focusing on the life and teaching of Jesus from the cultural and mental milieu into which his life was inserted.

The legacy of the biblical scholar Rudolf Bultmann (1884–1976) may illumine some of these issues. The burden of Bultmann's enquiries was a program of demythologizing or existential interpretation that called for the disavowal of the historical character of many biblical statements (like the second coming of Christ) and their recognition instead as myths that convey truths about the struggles, intentions, and possibilities of human existence. In the existential post-Bultmanian climate it became commonplace in Protestant thinking to assert that science tells us about the natural world (and in a more limited way about the psyche) but does not purport to deal in ultimate matters of human existence and destiny. Revelation, on the other hand, addresses itself precisely to these questions about human existence and destiny, its meaning and value and transformation. We do not expect the Bible to tell us about the structure of the atom or the nature of electromagnet waves by way of a protoscience. Nor do we expect science to articulate the meaning of life or define ultimate goals and values. On the contrary, a kind of modus vivendi has been worked out between explanatory thinking undertaken by science and the existentialist analysis and therapy (redemption) that is the focal concern of religion.

It is necessary to see the dangers of making revelational claims vulnerable to the discoveries of an ever-changing, evanescent science. The autonomy of revelation is maintained by restricting its purview to questions of human meaning and salvation and withdrawing it from the kind of explanatory hypotheses characteristic of science. A few of my Muslim informants and interlocutors were aware of these concerns and justified their apologetic enterprise by contending that while science cannot establish the truth of the Qur'an, it can nevertheless act as a confirmation of a Qur'anic truth. Again, however, there is a theological danger in tying one's revelation too closely to the transient and provisional nature of scientific propositions. It would seem that the course of wisdom is to make the existential and soteriological claims of revelation relatively independent of the revisable, hypothetico-deductive assertions of science. Otherwise there is the danger that the miraculous actions of the sovereign and gracious God will be transmuted into the mechanistic operations of inherent natural law, and, further, that the authority of revelation will be threatened by the subsequent scientific invalidation of statements that have been too closely associated with the essential revelational core.

I remain unclear as to the psychological impact of this Muslim anticipation of scientific statements within the Qur'an. One consequence might be the exclusion of Muslims from vigorous engagement in the scientific enterprise since all that would come to light in the long run would be insights that are already available to them, even though *in nuce*, in the Qur'an. The other quite contrary result might be to impel Muslims towards science on the same assumption that characterized the seventeenth-century deists in Europe, namely, that in engaging in science to uncover the operations of the natural world, they were only thinking God's thoughts after him. I can only speculate about which of these largely unconscious psychological effects is the case.

part one
COMMUNITY

LEFT: Syed Mahmud Ahmad, principal of Jamia Ahmadia, the theological college, in Rabwah

RIGHT: Eid prayers in Rabwah

LEFT: Ahmadis who give ten percent of their income during their lifetime and will ten percent of their estate to Ahamdiyyat are buried in this cemetery, which is seen as an honour. In the background is one of the many rock formations surrounding Rabwah

RIGHT: Nino with the director of education in Rabwah

 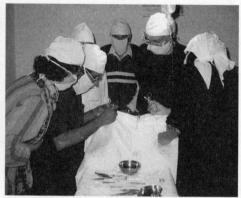

LEFT: The director of *langar kahna* showing Naseer and us the huge store-room where 225-pound sacks of rice, lentils, flour, and sugar are stored in hopsacking bags

RIGHT: The doctors of the Rabwah Hospital give up their one free day a week to spend twelve hours in the neighbouring countryside treating poor villagers. Few of the villagers, if any, are Ahmadi, yet none are charged fees. We were privileged to watch this cataract operation, one of many performed that day

CHAPTER TWO

Piety and Religious Practice in Rabwah

Peggy and I on a typical morning stuck our heads out the door of the bungalow to see what was happening to the sky. Earlier, in the predawn before the *azhan*, or call to prayer, when I first left our bedroom and went out the screen doors of the foyer into the courtyard, the stars had that intense brightness that only a black background can provide. When we emerged an hour or so later, the distant barren hills that dominate Rabwah and the cypresses that border the walk were serrated against the slowly lightening sky.

In spite of the *azhan* at 5:30 A.M., the grounds and village itself still seemed to be sound asleep. One wonders how many of the faithful actually frequent the *fajr*, or first prayer of the day, at the mosque. Of course they may be saying their prayers in the privacy of their own homes and no doubt the majority are. The Muslim ideal is to participate in the ritual prayer in a congregation, usually within about fifteen minutes of the call to prayer. Islam is flexible and reasonable, however, and there is latitude to perform the prayers in private, in one's office or home, or outside in the grounds, and within a reasonable amount of time so long as the prayers do not overlap with the subsequent prayer. In cases where it is difficult to meet the prayer obligations, it is usually possible to combine a missed prayer with the next scheduled devotions.

The next morning, I slid the heavy barrel bolts that hold the solid wooden door secure and stepped out into the blackness, still surprisingly opaque at six. I walked across the brick patio through the little gate and out onto the paved driveway in front of the Tarik offices, bordered with cypresses and rose bushes. The stars were not as sharp and visible this morning, although the dominant star in the East was still very prominent. There was something luxuriously sensual about strolling the driveways with my hot coffee in a hefty mug purchased at the bazaar yesterday to replace the small china teacups that are not adequate for the amount of coffee I enjoy in the morning.

Through the iron gates of the compound I could see in the gloom created by the streetlights the quickly moving figures of men in pairs, most of them draped in what I characterize as a typical Balti-style shawl but which is really a Punjabi shawl thrown in a romantic and masculine way around the shoulders. Bending forward against the chill air, the men were clearly hurrying to get to the mosque for the *salat*, or corporate prayers. It is noteworthy how marked piety still is in places like Rabwah, given the inconvenience of a discipline that requires prayer before the sun rises.

The power cut off at 6:00 A.M. and remained off for an hour and a half, which was a nuisance because it obliged me to work by candlelight. The dictating was easy but reading presented problems. The impediments posed by the power cuts, which amount to about seven prime hours during the working day (that is, excluding cuts during sleeping hours), were partially mitigated when an electrician hooked our bungalow up to a generator. But it requires the constant attention of the bearer and he sleeps later than I do, so I cannot benefit from it in the mornings. As I strolled out into the compound, I noticed the *chowkidars*, or watchmen, swathed in their shawls still sleeping in the passageways or cloisters of the foreign missions office. The introduction of a generator did mean that I was able to work during the day other than in the early morning, particularly during the evening power cuts when I wanted to read and write after dinner. I still had to work by candlelight in the early mornings.

Friday Prayer in Rabwah

Every Friday the faithful come from all over the community of Rabwah to the Jumma Masjid, the great central mosque, for the Friday noon prayer in which a sermon (*khutba*) is preached. On my first visit I walked up the long road, perhaps a mile or so, to the al-Aksa mosque and entered the grounds, which were chockablock with many hundreds of bicycles, motor scooters, motorcycles, and cars, in addition to the throngs of pedestrians making their way through the gates and into the mosque courtyard. I calculated afterwards that there was a minimum of six thousand to eight thousand people present. I sat near the front of the mosque on a rush mat with all the men. The women are in an upstairs balcony and off to the sides behind curtains and one never sees them.

The sermon runs about forty minutes and the Muslim prayer itself is quite brief, lasting only about seven minutes. Many people arrive early to say private prayers before the obligatory ritual prayer (*salat*) and stay behind afterwards to continue their private prayers, standing with hands upraised or arms folded, bowing, and kneeling in the customary Islamic postures (*rak'as*). The Ahmadi ritual prayer is identical to the Sunni prayer with this difference: the Ahmadi encourage their members to add their own personal supplications between the various elements of the prayer and again at the end. This is not to say that the Sunnis discourage this; but the Ahmadis have raised it to prominence among their members.

Upon returning from the mosque, I found Peggy sitting in the brick courtyard deeply engrossed in her book. It was a pleasant scene. I joined her and we sat in the mild sun and read. Later in the afternoon we walked down the road to the village shopping area, which is called Gol Bazaar, and strolled around its semicircular road bordering a central grassy island that has unfortunately been allowed to become quite derelict. Peggy held onto my arm out of a forty-year inexpungeable habit. It is normally unacceptable for Muslims to give any public demonstration of affection, but we thought that walking arm in arm was rather mild and would not likely give offence. A number of people called out *Assalam-o-Alaikum,* "Peace be with you," to which we replied *Walaikum-salam,* "Peace be upon you as well." They are used to seeing visitors here, but few of them are foreigners. In any case we received no hostile stares as one might get in some conservative Sunni Muslim milieux.

Most of the shops in the bazaar were closed because Friday has become a day of rest for Muslims, although the Qur'an does not stipulate that it is a pause day like the Jewish Sabbath or the one-time Christian Lord's Day. Muslims are obliged, however, to make every effort to attend the Friday noon prayer because it is one of the central acts of Muslim solidarity. Islam places great stress on the corporate, social, cultural, and political nature of the tradition, as well as on the inward and spiritual. Consequently, this act of congregational solidarity is symbolically important.

On another Friday Nasrullah Malahi, a young missionary designated for Uzbekistan in the former Soviet Union, picked me up at about 11:30 A.M. and we walked down the main shopping street to the Jumma Masjid. Though the sermon was not to start until 1:10, already large groups of people were thronging down the street to the mosque. We took our place inside, although by far the largest part of the congregation would be outside in the large courtyard and beyond; many worshippers during late winter and early spring prefer to be outside in the sun. We sat on the long straw mats that cover the mosque floor both inside the structure itself and outside in the courtyard.

The method of delivering the *khutba* is what I found most interesting. Because of the governmental prohibition on their use of loudspeakers, the Ahmadis have devised a human telegraphic system of getting the message from the *minbar*, or pulpit, at the front down to the last row hundreds of yards away. Ten men had the text of the sermon and they spread themselves at intervals both longitudinally and latitudinally throughout the congregation. When the preacher uttered a phrase it was repeated by the human telegraphers so that the audience within range of their voice would hear the sermon. The human voice transmitters had either to hear or guess when the preacher had finished a phrase. We could hear the various voices and except for one, which always seemed to trail off at the end, they were remarkably uniform. When the khalifa gives his sermons he likes to preach without a text, so the transmitters must hear every word in order to repeat it faithfully to the distant congregation. The sermon lasted about three-quarters of an hour, minus the repetitions.

Immediately following the *khutba*, the congregation moved into the Friday prayers, which consisted of two *rak'as*, or series of prostrations. Following this there were additional prayers for a person who had died the previous evening and whose body had been brought to the mosque. It has become apparent that veneration of the dead and the visitation of cemeteries to seek blessings and to bestow blessings upon the souls of the dead are an important part of Ahmadi devotional life. They hold the view that heaven is not a uniform place but has within it gradations. Prayers by faithful friends and family members on behalf of the dead will assist them to a higher state of spiritual development and proximity to God in heaven. In this respect it resembles the Roman Catholic practice of praying for the souls in purgatory although the analogy is only very general because the souls for whom the Ahmadis pray are conceived of as already in heaven, not in purgatory requiring the discharge of temporal consequences of sin.

The faithful in heaven can also work to achieve the spiritual well-being of those on Earth, although this is more exceptional. In special cases, God may grant to the devout souls in heaven the possibilities of appearance and intercession for those on earth. It is clear that the Muslims feel that with respect to the dead they are surrounded, in Christian language, by a host of witnesses.

Following the jumma prayer, I walked with Muhammad Ali, who was on the staff of the Theological Training School, to the Mubarak mosque, which used to be the main mosque in Rabwah until it was outgrown by the increase of population. But it retains a favoured place in the piety of the Ahmadis because three khalifas said their prayers there. The occasion of our visit was the practice of *itikawf*, which is a type of retreat that both men and women undergo during the last ten days of Ramadan. They seclude themselves, apart from the jumma prayer, in the mosque for that whole ten-day period taking their meals, their early-morning *sari* (food before the fast) somewhere around 4:00 or 4:30 in the morning, fasting the whole day, then breaking the fast with the *iftar* (food after the day's fast) at sunset. The day is spent in the five mandatory collective prayers, in private prayer and meditation, and in Qur'an and Hadith reading. Each person occupies a separate cell, which could more appropriately be called a tent. It reminded me of Jewish *sukkot*, the little huts built for the Festival of Booths to commemorate the wanderings in the wilderness. The "tents" are constructed by stringing long wires across one side of the mosque interior from which the individual participants in the retreat hang sheets, or *shamiana* drapes, to make a little cubicle, which is probably not much larger than six-by-eight feet. There they spread out a bed-roll and perhaps a little low table on which to place books. The purpose of the retreat is to remove oneself mentally as well as physically from the cares and ambitions of the everyday world in order to devote oneself exclusively to the praise of God and the supplication of his blessings.

I waited for Naseer, a returned missionary who served as our guide around Rabwah, to return from the jumma prayer and then we went into his little tabernacle to discuss the details of the practice of *itikawf*. A journalist from further south invited us to his cubicle where he photographed us together. The journalist expressed an interesting physiological interpretation of fasting saying that it burns away bodily toxins and thus purifies the body and moreover burns away human sin, thus purifying the person spiritually. This therapeutic value of fasting was corroborated later by Dr Latif Qureshi, director of internal medicine and cardiology at the Ahmadi Hospital in Rabwah, who reported that in the eleven months of the year preceding Ramadan, he gains about seven kilos, which he then loses throughout the fast of Ramadan, when in addition to fasting from dawn to sunset, he also reduces his food intake. He conceded that it is quite possible to end up eating as much or more by gorging oneself when one rises in the early morning or middle of the night to eat the *sari* and then by overindulging at *iftar* when one breaks the fast. Dr Qureshi's view is that we are not camels and that this practice is both physiologically mistaken and spiritually self-defeating since it deprives the faster of the discipline and the privation that is one of the benefits of fasting.

Although the men at the Mubarak mosque were in a quiet time of prayer and meditation, they seemed very interested in my visit. The word had got around that there was a visiting Canadian professor, accompanied by his wife, who had written a book on Ahmadis that had proved to be extremely useful to the community at large in presenting its legitimate nature and claims to a wider non-Ahmadi audience. In any case, the Ahmadis are a curious and extraordinarily hospitable community. One man insisted on giving me a brand-new copy of the Qur'an, despite my inability to read Arabic. I told him that his graciousness was not in vain because our daughter, who could read Arabic, would read it both for herself and to us.

The Celestial Cemetery

One morning Peggy and I accompanied Naseer to the Bahishti Maqbarah, the heavenly or paradisal cemetery, where he prayed at the grave of his parents. This is a special cemetery that contains the bodies of the *moosis*, or pledgers. These are persons who have vowed to donate one-tenth of their income and one-tenth of their legacy to the *jama'at*. The customary contribution of an Ahmadi to the *jama'at* is one-sixteenth of their income or six and one-quarter percent. This originates from the days when a rupee was made up of sixteen annas and the expected donation of the members of the *jama'at* was one annah per rupee of income.

The total number of *moosis* is in the area of thirty thousand. Some are buried in Qadian, in the Indian Punjab, but the vast majority are buried in Rabwah. The original intention was to move the coffins to Qadian, but after partition this seems less and less a possibility.

The custom of the pledge, or *wasiyyat*, goes back to a revelation that the Promised Messiah had in 1905, which is contained in a tract called "The Will." The Promised Messiah himself died in 1908 and the revelation of 1905 was an anticipation of his death and the scheme for the *wasiyyat*, or higher-level financial pledge, originates in that revelation. Some of the headstones contain the statement that the burial is only temporary. For example, on the gravestone of the wife of the Promised Messiah and mother of the second khalifa are inscribed the words "Buried temporarily, to be removed to Qadian."

The cemetery is clean and well designed with spacious walkways or boulevards through the sections of headstones. Each grave is indicated by a symmetrical heap of earth, generally covered with crushed stone that marks the length of the coffin, and a headstone. None of the headstones of rank-and-file devotees are large or ostentatious.

Inside the large cemetery compound there is another walled compound, with a gate and iron railing around the top, marking the area that contains the members of the family of the Promised Messiah. The most notable grouping consists of four large mosque-shaped headstones with arches. These contain, from left to right, the wife of the Promised Messiah, then with a larger monument the body of the second khalifa, next that of the third khalifa, and finally, marked again with a smaller structure, the wife of the third khalifa. Off to the right there is a headstone that serves as a memorial to the wife of the present khalifa, Mirza Tahir. Her body lies in the cemetery at Woking in Britain.

While we were examining these headstones and having the inscriptions translated for us, several Ahmadis came and stood reverently before the tombs, putting their hands forward with palms upward in the customary Ahmadi gesture of supplication, and said their prayers. Some of the inscriptions had been erased, in conformity with the prevailing law targetting the Ahmadis in Pakistan. Some of the erased epigraphs following the names of the khalifas were, "Peace be upon him." This was thought by the orthodox to be applicable only to the Prophet Muhammad and his family. Other erased epigraphs were "Mother of believers," and "May Allah be pleased with him." Those were all on the headstone of the second khalifa. On the marble incised headstone of the third khalifa, "Commander of the faithful" had been plastered over. Failure to do so would incur the risk of charges against the Ahmadis of posing as Muslims, by using phrases in their devotional life that the Sunnis, in collaboration with the government, have prescribed to be appropriate only to those who are Muslims. The ludicrous nature of this situation is seen in the fact that I, a foreign Christian, can use the phrase *Assalam-o-alaikum* – "Peace be with you" – a standard way in which all Muslims greet one another and say farewell to one another; while an Ahmadi in using the same greeting, would be liable to a criminal charge, fine, and imprisonment on the grounds, once again, of having posed as a Muslim or alternatively of having engaged in an action that is offensive to Muslims.

Naseer informed me that were the mullahs to incite a group of Sunnis to storm the cemetery walls or gate with the intention of desecrating the tombs, they would be resisted to the death by every Ahmadi man, woman, and child in Rabwah. The Ahmadis have a reputation for being, on the whole, an acquiescent group. There are for example, constant explosions from the solid rock mountain that overlooks the cemetery as road-building companies blast for rock and crushed stone to be used in road construction. The explosions frequently cause some rocks to fall into the cemetery, damaging the tombstones. The feeling is that this can be done with relative impunity because the peaceful Ahmadis will not bother to bring legal action against the contractors who have caused the destruction. With respect to any deliberate attempt to vandalize the grave, however, Naseer is quite confident that the Ahmadi reaction would be swift, violent, and sacrificial.

One afternoon we went with Naseer to the Dar-al-Ziafat, the hostel and *langar kahna*, or common kitchen and dining-room, adjacent to the Tahrik-i-jadid. We were met by the director, Malik Munawar Ahmad Javaid. A BA and BED, he had been a successful business man in Lahore with the largest bottling company for Shezan soft drinks. In 1982, however, he heard a sermon by the khalifa exhorting the members of the *jama'at* to dedicate themselves wholeheartedly and sacrificially to the work of the movement, whereupon he abandoned his career as a businessman and gave himself to full-time service in the *jama'at*. His first job was as a manager of the *Review of Religion*, in which I once published an article entitled "The Khalifa as a Sacred Person." When Malik was manager the *Review* was published out of Rabwah but was subsequently transferred to London. After the transfer he was placed in charge of the hostel, Dar-al-Ziafat. Although he had no experience in the specific logistics of managing a huge food-and-accommodation establishment, his general managerial experience coupled with his commitment to serving the cause enabled him to master the procedures very quickly.

He took us on a tour of the premises, the small dining-room where groups can meet or take tea and the large dining-room where anyone who arrives will be fed. I'm not sure how many hundreds could be fed in there. We proceeded to the kitchen that served the large dining-room and then on into the storerooms. Malik opened three storerooms for us. The first contained numerous sacks of flour that must have weighed at least one hundred pounds each, resembling those sacks that I used at one time to manhandle when Peg was seriously into baking bread. Another room contained bags of the same size full of chickpeas, lentils, and other types of pulse. Yet another storeroom contained enormous bags of milk powder from the Republic of Ireland.

These sacks of food were stacked almost to the ceiling. Javaid told us that there was enough of a stock there for six months. We then moved into the chapati bakery. These are unleavened whole-wheat flat breads. Unfortunately the chapati machine, which is their pride, was not in operation as the machine is used only to feed large groups. These automatic or semi-automatic chapati machines and ovens can easily grind out enough chapatis to feed two thousand people in an hour or so. An enormous vat with a motor-driven mixer filled with flour, water, and oil is the starting point of the operation. The uncooked chapatis are then run on automated belts through the ovens and come out on the other side. We moved on to the kitchen, which can prepare food for thousands of people in short order. Gas jets are set into the floor over which are mounted enormous pots in which the dal and curry are cooked. These raging hot pots are carried by two men on bamboo poles to the place where the food is served. We then moved on to the abattoir. The Ahmadis do not buy their meat; instead they buy their animals, sheep and goats that they slaughter themselves.

At the back of the compound there are two stories of bedrooms. There were hundreds of charpois lined up along the walls. If the meetings coincide with the hot weather, the charpois are moved out onto the vast lawn in order to get the evening coolness. The whole place was extraordinarily clean and tidy. The lawns were manicured, the walks carefully swept and the buildings primly whitewashed. The hostel exudes a sense of organization, competence, and commitment, especially since most of it is run by volunteers or very marginally paid labour. Malik reported that on a couple of hours notice he could feed two thousand people chapatis and *dal*, a lentil-and-chickpea porridge that is scooped up with broken pieces of chapati or nan.

We could not prolong our tour because prayer time had arrived at 5:55. We went outside into the courtyard, where one young man was calling out the time for prayer. The straws mats were placed at one side of the lawn and the ranks of prayers assembled there. Just prior to the beginning of the prayer there was excitement as a cluster of men stood off to one side and pointed up to the sky and then raised their open palms upward in an attitude of prayer. Peggy and I went over to ascertain the cause of this perturbation and learned that it was the first visible appearance of the new moon. Although technically the new moon had been born the day before, it had not been visible to the naked eye above the horizon. Only tonight could it be seen and this officially marked the beginning of Ramadan. Because sunset had already occurred, it meant that eating could take place and the fast would begin with the next day's first light. Peggy and I sat by for the prayer, which takes very little time, perhaps seven minutes or so. We then walked slowly through the dusty gloom to our bungalow.

The Regimen of Ramadan

We were awakened at about 3:00 in the morning by a loud siren, which we had not heard the night before. It served to inaugurate Ramadan (the obligatory month of fasting that is one of the pillars of Islam) and as a wake-up signal for those who wanted to prepare some food and eat before the fast started at dawn, that is to say, before the sun rose. This was followed by about half an hour of Qur'an recitation broadcast at maximum volume over amplified loudspeakers from the Sunni mosques. This middle-of-the-night call was new and we connected it with Ramadan and the middle-of-the-night eating before the fast began. There seems to be little sense of private space. What would be considered an intrusion upon a private right to solitude and peace at home is here simply taken for granted with all the various Sunni mosques giving the call to prayer on their own time. The Ahmadis are, of course, forbidden by law to give the *azhan*, so what the Ahmadi children do instead is circulate in their own neighborhoods, chanting praises to God and to Muhammad at the top of their lungs as only young Pakistani children are able to do. This serves as a kind of a wake-up call and summons to prayer for their neighbours.

Once Ramadan had begun Peggy and I experienced a totally different Rabwah. As we walked to the bazaar in the late afternoon, the streets were almost deserted, without the customary crush of pedestrians, cars, cyclists, motorcycles, tongas, and donkey-carts. During Ramadan the whole pace of life slows right down. Paradoxically, a festive culinary side to life emerges. We noted that food stands had sprung up where they had not existed before. They were already getting into business with great spherical vats of boiling oil in which samosas and pakorahs were prepared as well as jalebi, the orange-coloured pretzel-type sweet that is squirted into the oil in artistic lacey shapes, quickly deep-fried, lifted out with a spatula, and dunked into another tub of either honey or sugared water, and then put on a drying rack. The merchant watched Peggy and me stand with great interest at this production and offered us a piece to taste. We had had jalebi before in central India, so we did not buy any then but we planned to relinquish the evening meal that was brought to us from the *langar kahna* (communal kitchen), which had become a little boring in recent days, and go down to the bazaar to buy samosas and pakorahs and jalebies from the stalls. The Islamic way of life with its mandatory communal ritual prayer is hard on normal patterns of sleep. Some periods of the year are not so trying because dawn comes later and evening sooner. Nevertheless, this middle-of-the-night piety at full volume is something new to cope with. This way of life is not made for sleeping in, at least not for those of us who do not have the skills to go back to sleep after the prayer time as many of our Pakistani friends do.

The *chowkidars* had already lit their pail full of brush and twigs to create the illusion of warmth in the early morning. Usually when I am doing my circuits they have not yet gotten around to it, but it was smouldering this morning when I started out and by the fifth circuit the flame was burning briskly out of the top of the bucket.

The Ahmadis frequently stress the reasonableness and flexibility of their devotional regimen in order to thwart any imputation that Islam is a dogmatic and fanatical religion. Fasting requirements during Ramadan are a case in point. We were told by Hiba, a precocious and sweet eleven-year-old, and her friend Fawza, also eleven, that they were not fasting because their parents considered them too young. They said that one girl in their class of the same age was fasting, but on closer questioning, it turned out that she fasted for only the first day or two and then resumed her normal eating schedule. Fawza's brother was also fasting, though he was only thirteen. But again it turned out that he would probably fast only for the first week because of his age. Hiba also explained that there is a kind of minifast for young children to follow with their parents' agreement. She used the Urdu word for "little sparrow." In this children's fast, the noon meal is taken and then no further food until after sunset. Food is also taken in the early morning before dawn. In this way children are gradually introduced to the discipline and rigours of fasting until they are old enough and strong enough to endure the full thirty days, at which time they are already accustomed to its sensations and trials and also its inner spiritual satisfaction.

Everyday activities slow substantially during Ramadan. We wondered whether productivity in Pakistan dropped to half its normal level in that month. It is hard to extrapolate from the Ahmadi instance because so much of their time and energy goes into their Islamic ritual observances and their educational pursuits, particularly during Ramadan. Every day they gather in one of the public buildings, the library or the men's headquarters or the youth organizational centre or the ladies' Anjuman building, in order to look at television, which is fed from satellite dishes above the buildings. From 4:30 to 6:00 every afternoon they view Hazoor's commentary on the Qur'an transmitted from London. We wonder how he is able to gear himself up every day for thirty days for a fresh presentation of Qur'anic commentary.

Hiba, the young neighbour girl, came by in the afternoon to get her picture taken and she reported that her father did not want me to put the story about the sparrow fast in my book, saying it's all imaginary. I think

I know what he was getting at. He had a very strong sense of what is authentically Islamic and proper and was apprehensive that I would go away with folktales masquerading as genuine Islam. I asked Hiba whether young children actually fasted, ate at noontime and then not again until sunset and then got up early in the morning in order to eat before they started the fast at dawn. If people did, it was not imaginary and I told Hiba to assure her father that I would not for a moment confuse this with normative Islam but that I viewed it as one of the lovely customs that have grown up in order to introduce children to both the concept and the discipline of the fast, including the discomfort of fasting. The abstinence is introduced gradually until they reach the age of maturity, when they can pursue the fast for the whole period from dawn till sunset.

The Anjuman treasury gong sounded six times as I sat reading luxuriously by electric light since the power cuts had been eliminated. Whether this was just in honour of Ramadan or whether the power situation had objectively improved, I do not know. I rose about 5:00 A.M. after a somewhat restless night and began my walk just as the 5:35 call to prayer sounded simultaneously with the long siren by which the municipal council announces the beginning of the fast. This is dawn only by the operation of the most fervent imagination. Were it not for the neon lights surrounding the entrance of the administration building near our bungalow, total darkness would prevail. The dominant eastern star still shone brightly and the air was cool and refreshing. According to the Sunni, the morning call to prayer (*fajr*) comes when there is sufficient light to distinguish a white thread from a black thread. I keep looking at my white finger over against my dark purple jacket and trying to determine whether or not I could pass that test. Ahmadis have a different construction and they take the threads to mean the first upwards rays of the sun as the light begins to appear above the horizon even though the sun is still well below the horizon. It is hard to determine precisely where the horizon is because of the rock mountains that surround Rabwah. Since they are being systematically quarried for road building, it may not be long before Rabwah too is just a flat gravel plain, except for those spots where irrigation remains. After I completed three circuits, I was just able to discriminate the bulk of the east mountain against the sky. This had to serve as a test that dawn was indeed present. Sunrise was at about 7:45. Two women came out of the corner of the compound, from the housing settlements that accommodate many staff workers and their families. I wondered if they were strolling for exercise as I had seen a few others do that early in the morning, but I did not think this likely. As they went out the front gate, I realized they were on their way to the Mubarak mosque for prayers. As I passed them, I did not say *assalam-o-alaikum*, which I felt was awkward and unfriendly on my part, but neither did they initiate a greeting, which I would not have expected. Peggy and I had decided that it would be inappropriate for a lone man to greet women, certainly unaccompanied women, on the street, even with religious greetings.

On another afternoon, the siren announced the end of fast at 5:49 followed by the first *azhan*. I noted that Sharif (our bearer) and the chowkadar were breaking their fast together sitting on the charpoi in the main driveway and sharing their food, which was placed on newspaper spread between them. Sharif gesticulated in a way that was reminiscent of peasants eating by the side of the road in Sicily; they would say "*Favorisci*" if you happened to pass by, meaning, "Please honour us by joining us." This may have been a pro forma social ritual that one was not normally expected to accept, but it showed a deep civility. I just shook my head, smiled at Sharif, and politely declined. At the distance I could not see what they were going to break the fast with but I noted there were a couple of oranges. This was not the heavy meal of the day, which would follow later.

These are very busy days for the Ahmadis. They gather for Hazoor's daily *dars*, or expository lesson on the Qur'an, which comes by satellite transmission from London. It runs from 4:30 to 6:00 P.M. but since the signal for the end of the fast comes at approximately 5:49, the people break the fast with samosa or pakorah and, as is the practice according to custom of the Prophet, a date and some water, even while the teaching continues on the live telecast. When the telecast ends they have just enough time to walk to the mosque of their choice – there are approximately forty Ahmadi mosques scattered throughout the municipality. The two principal ones are close by the headquarters compounds and there the prayers begin at 6:10 P.M. – a little later than usual thanks to allowances made for Ramadan. After this they have just enough time to go home and eat their dinner before leaving for their ablutions and evening prayers. The busy Ramadan schedule is compounded by the addition (certainly for the pious) of a number of extra prayers. The primary focus during Ramadan, certainly amongst the Ahmadi Muslims in Rabwah, seems to be on the performance of ritual duties, as life orbits around the schedules imposed by the observance of mandatory and voluntary rituals, especially prayers.

On a couple of mornings I went down the street to the Gol Bazaar and then to the tailor to see if my *shalwar kameez* was finished. The shops were busy, indicating a fairly full business life though not as full as on other days. The butcher shop was doing a thriving trade as the butcher hacked off chunks from the hanging legs of two large sheep and then chopped them up on the blocks for various customers. It appeared that some people had been making special efforts to feed their families more festive fare at the end of the fast day or just before the beginning of the fast in the early morning. As I have indicated, a siren goes off just before three o'clock in the morning throughout the town. It is sponsored by the municipal council, none of whom happen to be Ahmadis, though Ahmadis constitute ninety-five percent of the population in Rabwah. The siren is followed by some recitation over the loudspeakers though not yet the *azhan* because it is not yet dawn. People are alerted to arise at this time and prepare food if they wish, in order to be ready to start the fast with the dawn.

Dr Latif Qureshi told us that the exemption from the fast while one is traveling (or ill) does not amount to a total exemption. The missed fast days must subsequently be made up either by fasting on the days when one is not traveling or ill, once Ramadan is over, or by feeding the poor with the food that one would not have consumed had one engaged in the fast. Latif's aged mother in fact did that. Because of her age she was exempt from the fast in the literal sense but still met its moral and spiritual requirements by giving food to the poor and thereby meeting the spiritual intention of the divine ordinance to fast.

EID-AL-FITR

The Ahmadi community could scarcely have had a more beautiful day for the celebration of the Eid-al-Fitr, which marks the closing of the Ramadan month of fasting.

We were driven to al-Aqsa mosque. The streets were plugged with people winding their way towards the mosque. It must be that just about every man, woman, and child from Ahmadi families in Rabwah was present at the Eid prayer with the exception of the single member of the family who, in at least seventy-five percent of the homes, was left behind to provide security against vandalism or arson.

It was almost mind-boggling to see the throngs winding their way up the long access street and through the main gate of the grounds and along the drive that leads to the mosque proper. Already in the access street, the lines started to diverge, women walking on one side of the road separated by a line of young men, while the men walked on the other. The *khutba* was scheduled to start at 8:30 but the enormous crowds disrupted the normal schedule and the service was a little late starting. The majority of women were dressed in their white or black burqas, which hid the garments that they wore underneath: otherwise the place would have been a blaze of colour. Beneath the hem of the burqas one could still see a foot or so of flashing colourful *shalwar* as the women strode purposely towards the mosque. Some young girls wore frilly little frocks that reminded me of nothing so much as Catholic first communion in a Calabrian hilltown. Black burqas and black headscarfs still predominated, although some had switched to a summer beige and to white. A very small minority of women appeared without any puritanical burqa, although with head and even face covered with a *dupatta* and veil.

The sky was crystalline blue, the warm sun beating on our backs as we sat on the vast lawns in front of the al-Aqsa mosque. Naseer had brought a rolled straw mat, which we spread on the ground in order to protect ourselves from the grass and the earth. The announcement came over the loudspeaker that the service was about to start, but still the throngs made their way into the mosque courtyard. We stood in one of the long files that spread from one side of the grounds to the other – a distance of at least a quarter of a mile. The first part of the worship was broadcast over loudspeakers. After the prayer, I took a stroll along the pathway that intersects this large prayer ground, observing that some people had already dispersed. There was an inducement to leave due to the difficulty of hearing the sermon thanks to the prohibition on amplification. The loudspeaker was in fact employed for the ritual prayer (*salat*) and for the Arabic recitation that prefaced the sermon, but once the sermon itself started the amplification had to be turned off.

It should be pointed out the prohibition of the use of loudspeakers for the *khutba*, which applied first, and for a long time only, to the Ahmadis, had been extended to all congregations. Certain mullahs were giving inflammatory speeches from their mosque loudspeakers that targeted the Shi'a and caused heavy violence and murder particularly in Karachi. This finally prompted the government to prohibit these incendiary sermons that were causing Pakistan to disintegrate into sectarian strife.

As I stood at the edge of one of the courtyard laneways the sermon continued in the relay system that I first encountered at the previous week's jumma service. Where Naseer and his sons and I were sitting, it was impossible to grasp the relayed sermon. No doubt some people would have left even if they had been able to hear: it was still a thriving business day in the streets and the displays of sweets for sale were a work of art reminiscent of the way the Christmas markets in Bangalore, India, were decorated with mounds of colourful fruit. Presently a young man stationed himself beside me, curious about the stranger who was dictating into a cassette player. There was a high security consciousness because of the everpresent threat of spies or police informers. The vigilant eavesdropper was undoubtedly trying to ascertain whether I represented a danger to the community.

I sat by the gas stove with Peggy on another early morning having my second cup of coffee by candlelight. I had awakened well before dawn and finally got up with the *azhan* at about 5:30. The Sunni *azhan* had already sounded but I had not reacted to it. The power was still on so I boiled some water for coffee. I strolled about the drive until the power cut out after 6:00. The harsh, neon light that surrounded the entrances to the administration building was replaced by the full-moon glow and starlight; one of which beams with great intensity over the mountain to the east of us.

The *chowkidar* was hawking and splashing in the little servant's bathroom in the corner of our compound. As I strolled, I became aware of a group of children singing lustily and loudly, almost yelling out their lyrics. I can only suppose that they were singing religious songs, equivalent to Hindu *bhajans*. I don't know whether almost everyone is up at this time in response to the call for the *fajr* prayer or whether there simply is little of the sense of public space and public decorum that imposes Anglo-Celtic restraints on intrusion into the private lives of others.

I find it a distinct luxury to stroll back and forth on the drive alongside the hedges and tall cypresses in that chilled, dark morning air with my hot mug of coffee in my hand. In the almost two weeks since we arrived at Rabwah, the morning light had increased noticeably. Gradually the days were getting longer and the air warmer.

In Islamabad Peggy and I visited the enormous Shah Faisal mosque, which is undoubtedly the largest mosque in Pakistan, larger even than the Bad Shahi in Lahore. Designed by a Turkish architect, it is characterized by its four ICBM minarets at each corner, which I find rather disturbing, although the interior hall is entrancing with its repetition of the Bedouin tent motif. The interior is a freestanding structure unsupported by columns with cantilevered arches meeting at the keystone in the centre. We walked on the marble floors of arcades that surround the prayer hall. Some of the arcades were in the shade, providing attractive cloisters in which to bring one's books and spend the day in meditation and study. In fact quite a few students from the adjacent Islamic University do just that. I can only guess that in synthesizing missile minarets with the Bedouin tent, the architect was trying to symbolize both the modern and the archaic dimensions of Islam.

CHAPTER THREE

Social Life and Institutions

The Khalifa

One Friday Peggy and I had a video interview for Ahmadiyyat TV. Afterwards we adjourned for tea to another studio and watched the televised
Friday sermon, given in Urdu, of the now-deceased Khalifatul Masih IV,
or Hazoor, as he was affectionately called by his devotees. Peggy and I
were instantly seized by an impression of fatigue and age that seemed to
have overtaken Hazoor since we last met him several years ago. This did
not surprise us given the inhuman load of responsibility that is placed
upon the khalifa. Every one of his devotees wishes to have a personal
connection with the khalifa. This is entirely consistent with the presuppositions of their belief system because the khalifa is a divinely given
conduit between God and the community of believers on earth.

The function of the khalifa, and especially the Ahmadi khalifa who
continues to have disclosures from God, is essential in bridging the
divine-human gulf. As a consequence enormous personal demands are
made upon the khalifa. People will ask him to choose a name for their
unborn child. Because of the great emphasis put on dreams as a medium
of communication from God in the Ahmadi worldview, Hazoor receives
many requests for dream interpretation. These he deals with. Ahmadi

missionaries are obliged to report fortnightly and their reports go directly to Hazoor, who finds time to read them since people judge their own
situations by his reactions – sometimes chiding and at other times encouraging – and by his instructions. He is beseeched daily by hundreds of
requests for prayers for the healing of the sick, guidance, choices of marriage mates, the vocational choices of children – any matters that concern
the lives of the devotees are brought before Hazoor for his judgment and
blessing.

The present khalifa is also a *hakim*, or specialist in homeopathy, so he
receives many requests for homeopathic diagnosis and treatment. How
he is able to deal with this avalanche of duties and requests and petitions
baffles us. We are told that he sleeps perhaps two to four hours nightly
and is therefore able to do what ordinary people cannot find time to do:
his energy is seen as a sign of divine favour. He was, and perhaps still is,
a vigorous walker. We cannot escape the impression that the system is
gravely top-heavy with expectations of the spiritual leader that might
have been appropriate to a much smaller and more cohesive community
but is no longer workable in an increasingly organized and worldwide
religious movement.

Additionally, Hazoor leads the *salah*, or obligatory prayers, all five
times during the day. This means that he has to be up and ready to lead
prayer, depending on the time of year, from at least five o'clock onward
and until quite late at night. Moreover, he is responsible for the weekly
Friday sermon. He gives many audiences to devotees and engages in a
program of public speaking. In short, we confront a situation of enormous – perhaps excessive – responsibility devolving upon the leader.

One afternoon I had tea with Naseer, our liaison and guide. As we sat out on
the patio in front of our bungalow, a curious incident occurred. Looking
distressed, Naseer arose from his seat and went to where Peggy or I had laid
some books from a little table on the ground, leaning them against the side
of the building. We had done this in order to make room for the tea tray. He
pushed the tray to one end of the small table and then took the books from

the ground and placed them on the table. He had obviously been distressed that books were being treated in what might be a disrespectful way.

Later that evening when he came to visit again, I said to him that in one of the books by Hazoor, there were numerous quotations in Arabic from the Qur'an and enquired whether this above all else was what had distressed him, since the Qur'an is to be treated only with the greatest sanctity. He had not known that there were Qur'anic quotations in that particular book. Rather, it was the principle of derogation of the quality of the book itself that had bothered him. No doubt he would have been even more profoundly upset had he realized that passages from the Holy Book had been laid on the ground.

Naseer testified to the particular sanctity that inheres in the town of Rabwah. Three of the khalifas spent time there, as well as many of the companions of the khalifas. Additionally there are the cemeteries that contain the remains of the khalifas and their spouses and some of the illustrious companions of the khalifas during the early spread of Ahmadiyyat. Consequently there is a sense that one is in a special spiritual environment here, not least because of the many prayers that have been uttered in this locale, prayers that have caused the very buildings and landscape to be pervaded by special access of the divine presence.

Contemporary Ahmadis have tremendous love for Hazoor and feel in return that his love and guidance flow out towards them. Their connection with the divine is maintained in large measure through their connection with the spiritual head of the community.

This is not illogical because even in their ordinary affairs, devotees discover how persons can be instruments of divine blessing, redemption, and joy. It is through these human instrumentalities that sacred reality makes its approach to humans and Hazoor manifests this familiar human phenomenon in a particularly acute way.

The experience of our friend Ijaz illustrates the relationship between the Ahmadis and Hazoor very well. Ijaz practised law in the United Kingdom, enjoying a prosperous barrister's life with a home in Rye, from which he could commute comfortably to London. The then khalifa, visiting the UK, said to him at a meeting, "You left your father a lonely man." This immediately raised the possibility in Ijaz's mind that he was not doing the right thing by remaining in England, but the khalifa gave no express direction as to what course of action he should pursue. Subsequently, however, the khalifa sent a message through Zafrulla Khan that he should return to Pakistan. This order of the khalifa came on 6 August and by 19 August Ijaz was back in Pakistan. He had sold his house and returned to Pakistan without even waiting for all the financial arrangements to be completed. On the orders of the khalifa he returned not to his parental home in Lahore but to Islamabad where he was then instructed to settle.

Ijaz was not certified to practise law in Islamabad but only in the Lahore area. The resolution was that he would seek a place in government service. He applied for one job after the application deadline had expired but he importuned his would-be employers into giving him an interview and was given the job because of his superior capacities. Within hours, however, the employer received a phone call from an important official requesting the position for his friend and Ijaz lost the job. He was staying in the Ahmadi guesthouse when a servant brought him the newspaper – not one of the usual amenities – and upon opening it he spotted an advertisement for a position with the Monopoly Commission at twice the salary. He applied for it and got the job. All of these events – from the khalifa's visit to London to the phonecall that caused him to be rejected for the first public service job, to the advent of the servant with the newspaper advertising the second job – all of these Ijaz, whose name means miracle, saw as the providential leadings of God in pursuit of his merciful divine purposes for his faithful devotees in response to the khalifa's intercessory prayers. Among the Ahmadi such piety is commonplace and is the hallmark, I believe, of Ahmadi commitment. God not only exists but is powerfully involved in the needs of his faithful people and acts to serve their highest interests in this life and the next.

The role of the khalifa is difficult to fathom for those raised in liberal democratic traditions. The khalifa is seen as the link between the holy and almighty God and the community. He exercises guidance because of the special spiritual grace that God bestows on the khalifat. The devotees' responsibility is quickly, simply, happily to obey the khalifa's instructions.

Founder Mirza Ghulam Ahmad's rhapsodies on the prophet Muhammad could serve with a simple change of name as Christian hymns of praise for their devotional attachment to the Lord Jesus. In the Ahmadi case the attachment is augmented by devotion to the Promised Messiah, who is seen as exemplary spiritual figure and normative interpreter of Qur'anic revelation and recipient of derivative revelation. To this is further added emotional attachment to and reliance upon the successive khalifas. Phenomenologically, it is difficult to escape the conclusion that human beings are structurally disposed towards the need for mystic seers, revelatory prophets, and succouring redeemers to deal with the existential assault upon them of meaninglessness, moral failure and guilt, finitude and death. In the face of their own inexpungeable weakness people transfer their hopes and loyalties to charismatic figures who are able to do with their supernatural power what they would otherwise be incapable of. Such sacred persons are also needed to introduce into everyday life the sacred mystery and numinous presence that would otherwise escape fallible and ordinary human perceptions.

In his book about the northwest frontier, *Lords of the Khyber*, André Singer tells of the numerous insurrections that kept the British busy in Afghanistan and on the Indian side of the Khyber Pass. The insurrections in many instances were led by radical (the British would have said fanatical) Muslim leaders such as the Faquir of Ipi or the Mad Mulla of Powindah. These religious leaders were able to garner large followings to rebel against British control because of the people's allegiance to Islam in the first place but also because of their own charismatic power and oratorical eloquence. Some of them were exemplary in the ascetical and pious conduct of their personal lives. One of the reasons they were able to marshal such widespread support against the British army was the magical powers that were ascribed to them. British bullets were said to bounce harmlessly off the bodies of the Pushtun tribesman, while the rocks that they threw into the air would turn into lethal hailstones against the British enemy as a result of the supernatural powers that could be evoked by the Muslim tribesmen.

This phenomenon of reliance on supernatural powers to deal with human problems is a cross-cultural occurrence. Even in my own erstwhile experience as a parish minister I often felt uncomfortable and inadequate when faced with parishioners' reliance on my presumed superior piety or wisdom in dealing with personal and pastoral problems. The Ahmadi community very quickly confronts us with their absolute confidence in the khalifa's ability to guide them in all difficult life choices. The khalifa embodies the vocation of the sacred person who either intrinsically possesses or has access to divine powers to deal with life's difficulties, from starvation to infertility, from natural catastrophe to national oppression. By this means the devotees acquire a sense of control and a power in what would otherwise be a situation of weakness, incapacity, and hopelessness. Where earthly and sacred persons with redemptive and charismatic power are absent, then this same need is addressed by appealing to supernatural presences either in the form of images or invisible or angelic spirit helpers. It occurs even in Protestant circles where the prevailing mythology is that superstition has been expunged in favour of individual freedom and individual faith. In fact the kind of status, wisdom, and authority ascribed to Pentecostal preachers by the incredulous faithful is but another instance of people's willingness to arrogate their self-determination to an external authority in order to acquire some sense of mastery over what would otherwise be the unbearable burden of unresolvable dilemmas.

I myself in these matters resonate to Nietzsche's appeal to love one's fate (*amor fati*), that is, heroically to accept the human struggle realizing that in many instances there is no way out, at least no way that conforms to human utopian fantasies. The eschatological impulse, however, resides deep within the human psyche and one can certainly sympathize with this transcendent hope in the face of overwhelming challenges and assaults. One need fear no evil because supernatural grace and power are, through one instrumentality or another, available to deal with that which one cannot in one's own might. But since the charismatic spiritual leader, miracle worker, guru, saint, or rescuer often turns out to be cast from the same fragile human clay from which we all emerge, this utopian reliance on another appears to be a highly problematic way of proceeding in the face of life's problems and perplexities. Having laid bare my humanist and secular proclivity, I have, nevertheless to confess that in the face of very grave illness I was glad to have the khalifa's prayers for my recovery. Among the many preachers, gurus, swamis, monks, and teachers that we have met over the years, the khalifa remains one of the few for whom we felt unqualified respect.

Majlis Ansarullah

When I visited the men's organization, or Majlis Ansarullah, Peggy did not join me, thinking that it might be inappropriate for her to attend. When I got there, however, Hamidullah, the national president of the Ansarullah, asked where Peggy was. Since a similar scruple had prevented me from going with Peggy to visit the women's organization, the Lejna, we thought, *mutatis mutandis*, that she should not go to the men's organization. In fact they do make allowances for non-Muslim foreigners and expect them, within limits of course, to abide by their own religious and cultural rules. I suspect that sometimes they are disappointed not to enjoy Peggy's buoyant and effervescent presence.

We had an interview of about an hour and a half. Much time was spent dealing with the structure of the organization, a matter that is not of great importance to me except for what it may reflect about the ethos of the Ahmadi movement. He wished to stress the democratic nature of the men's organization because I think they are sensitive to my characterization in *Conscience and Coercion* of the movement as hierarchical and authoritarian, which no doubt it essentially is. This coexists with democratic structures that ensure the election of local presidents of the men's organization and of a national president every three years. Together the presidents nominate an executive, which is approved by the membership at large.

Ansarullah has four main aims. The first is simply to maintain the organization. Survival is the natural drive of all institutions and bureaucracies, so the members are pledged to work for Ansarullah's well-being.

The second aim is the education of members. They are given a study syllabus that is prepared for every quarter and deals basically with the Qur'an and with the Founder's books. Hamidullah showed me a copy of the study booklet in Urdu titled *Heavenly Signs* dealing with the prophecies of the advent of the Promised Messiah. Their educational efforts are also dedicated to translating the Arabic prayers into Urdu. I was surprised to learn that many people, particularly in the villages, learn the five daily Arabic prayers by rote in childhood but do not know their literal meaning in their own language. Ansarullah's educational function is carried on partly at home with the help of the study booklets, with which every member is encouraged to familiarize himself, and partly at the monthly meetings, which are perhaps only an hour and a half long.

The third aim is what Hamidullah called training, which merges with the educational function and does not seem to be clearly distinguished.

The fourth is preaching: the members are encouraged to spread the word of Ahmadiyyat. The typical way of doing this is through one-on-one encounters with friends, business acquaintances, and work companions, and also through more public meetings that are still generally held in homes. The Ahmadis do not go in for the mass evangelistic type of rally, partly because in the present political context it would incur enormous anger and no doubt public protest marked with violence.

The Ahmadi evangelistic technique, if I may use the term metaphorically, resembles that of certain conservative Christian groups that stress the necessity of personal witnessing to friends. It also has affinities with the Frank Laubach system of literacy, which was patterned on the epigram "each one teach one" whereby anyone who was taught to read would then be under obligation to teach one other person to read. I had thought that the early Ahmadi movement stressed public preaching but Hamidullah told me that the movement never did emphasize this means of outreach. I had thought that the original debate between Mirza Ghulam Ahmad and the Christian missionaries and the exponents of the Hindu Arya Samaj were large public gatherings in which the contestants took each other on in the hope of exposing the weaknesses and foolishness of their opponents' arguments before a mass crowd. In fact, these were largely written debates where they would write their positions and their rebuttals back and forth.

In addition to the monthly meetings of Ansarullah, there is an annual *shura*, or consultative council meeting. Every particular *jama'at*, or local congregation, has its own *shura*. In addition there is a national *shura*, whose recommendations are submitted to the khalifa for his comments and ultimate approval. The *shura* is the ultimate court of authority, apart from the khalifa himself. Formerly all the various national *shuras* were organized into an international *shura*, or council, with its headquarters in Rabwah, but in 1989 the khalifa decided to decentralize and to constitute national *shuras* that reported directly to the khalifa and no longer to the international *shura* headquartered in Rabwah.

Ansarullah places stress on social service. For example, it runs free medical camps, particularly out in the countryside and villages. With their donations members have built a hospital in the Sind desert. They had intended to have it opened for the 1989 centenary, but they fell behind schedule. They had acquired twenty acres for the site and its construction was almost complete at the time of our last visit in 1995.

Funding takes place through donations called *chanda*, which are equivalent to one percent of gross monthly income. This is in addition to the one-sixteenth of their income (one-tenth if they wish to be buried in the heavenly cemetery) that members contribute to the *jama'at*. It is also in addition to their contribution to the expenses of the annual *jalsa*. It is clear that it is economically sacrificial to be an Ahmadi. Of course if someone simply has no income whatsoever, these various contributions are waived but the expectation is that even the poor will give proportionally out of whatever limited means they have.

The exposition of Qur'an and Hadith and the writings of the Promised Messiah, which is in fulfillment of the educational prong of the Ansarullah program, also takes place during the *dars*, which is the teaching that occurs after the set prayers, particularly the morning *fajr* prayer. When I attended morning prayers in Lahore, I noticed that following the ritual prayer, which takes perhaps seven minutes, some left, but a number would gather around the imam, in this case the locally appointed missionary, to hear his readings of the Qur'an and Hadith and to hear his exposition of those texts. The Ansarullah are encouraged to participate in the *dars* in order to deepen their understanding of Islamic faith and specifically the Ahmadiyyat interpretation of Islam.

In 1973 the third khalifa gave a strong urging that all the young people within 150 miles of Rabwah cycle to the *jalsa*, or annual meeting. He wished to see at least a thousand cyclists converge on Rabwah. The motivations were probably the health of the young people and also the encouragement of service. This was to be accomplished by getting the young people out into the villages. The khalifa felt strongly that many young people in Pakistan had no familiarity with their own country, particularly the village life. Hence the young people were encouraged to tour the villages in order to understand the conditions under which the majority of Pakistanis lived and to exercise their obligation to serve. They were to use these visits to teach the Qur'an on the grounds that this is shared with the Sunnis and so is common to all Muslims. The youth were specifically barred from preaching, the khalifa making a distinction between expositing the shared book of all Muslims and specific Ahmadiyyat proselytizing.

The khalifa said that all the junior or young members of Ansarullah, those forty to fifty-five, should own and use bicycles. That helps to explain the prominence of bicycles in Rabwah and their use by members of the staff of the various administrative offices. Most unexpectedly I was informed that the khalifa also urged cycling for ladies. I pointed out that I had not seen a single lady on a bicycle, other than one sitting adroitly on the back while her husband peddled. I was assured, however, that a few ladies still cycle.

Majlis Khuddam Ul-Ahmadiyya

I had a long and engaging interview at the youth organization, the Majlis Khuddam Ul-Ahmadiyya. My impression, quickly formed, was of the elaborate organizational structure of the youth organization. It should be borne in mind that in this context youth covers all young males from the ages of fifteen to forty. It is assumed that fifteen is the age at which maturity is attained and forty when mature paternal wisdom is acquired. I was presented with a copy of the organization's constitution which contains a complicated organizational structure and I will not at this point go into extensive detail.

The organizational apex is the national president who is elected by a national *shura*, or consultative body, and then confirmed by the khalifa. Under him there are districts that also have a leader, or *quaid*. Within a district there may be many local *jama'ats*, or chapters, and there are reported to be 950 chapters altogether in Pakistan. In very large *jama'ats*, the membership would be further broken down into a *halq*, a sector with a leader called *zaeem*. Until 1989 all the Khuddam associations throughout the world were under the authority of the office in Pakistan, but after a Friday sermon in 1989 in which the khalifa decentralized the authority, the president in Pakistan became responsible only for Pakistan. All other national presidents report directly to the khalifa. I am not clear what motivated the khalifa, but as the community spreads increasingly into the diaspora, it does seem appropriate to de-Pakistanize the movement.

The fundamental program of the Khuddam is set out in the pledge that all members take. It is essentially to train young males to develop morally and spiritually an Islamic identity and to serve God and the movement. There are sixteen departments each with its own secretary. Together the sixteen secretaries constitute the cabinet, which advises the *sadr*, or president. The national *sadr* with whom I spoke was Raja Muneer Ahmad Khan. With him was Mirza Ghulam Qadir, the secretary for the group. Raja Muneer is a tall well-built handsome man who carries himself with great dignity and disarming modesty. Mirza Ghulam is a highly articulate gentle-spirited person who seemed to be the quintessential academic type. He is in fact a computer scientist. The youth association started out mainly as a program of instruction in Qur'an and Hadith and in what we might call apologetics where young people are taught the details of Ahmadi faith and are instructed in how to respond to criticisms and win converts. This nowadays, given the constraining legislation upon Ahmadis that declares that it is a crime to proselytize, is limited to one-on-one personal testimony, as it is with the Ansarullah. The educational purpose of forming character and deepening faith is carried through by yearly program books and regular circulars that go out from the publication office of the headquarters in Rabwah. Where there is a resident missionary, he will assist the local Khuddam in this religious education. In other cases it is deputed to whichever member of the group is considered most able to do it.

Another department of the Khuddam deals with social service. In 1993–94 members ran 349 free medical camps in which 57,279 patients were seen. Over CDN $115,600 worth of free medicine was distributed. Like those run by the Ansarullah, the medical camps are conducted by volunteer doctors who go on their days off to see patients who would otherwise be deprived of medical attention. They also run a free eye camp on the same pattern. The ambulance service provided by the youth group is available to everyone in the community, not just Ahmadis. They also run a blood-donor clinic and have been responsible for the establishment of a blood bank in Rabwah.

One department deals with physical fitness. This is an important dimension of the youth program and the youth association boasts the largest public space in Rabwah. One of the difficulties faced by Ahmadis, at least potentially, is physical harassment and attack, so I asked whether there was any stress on martial arts instruction. I learned that they do in fact have some judo classes, but they lack qualified instructors.

Another dimension of the program is "dignity of labour." This was especially important to the second khalifa and it continues what Protestant Christians in the West would call work camps, or work bees. The roads in Rabwah were originally built by members of the youth organization and also by the Ansarullah. There are many fine trees in Rabwah, which was originally an arid desert region. This is also largely the result of planting carried out under the "dignity of labour" movement among the Khuddam and the Ansarullah. The youth gather to clean mosques, streets, and even the drains of the streets. They also run driving and typing schools. The general intention seems to be to provide uplifting services and to break down the strict hierarchical barriers that plague the subcontinent and ensure that manual labour is regarded as a contemptible activity fit only for people of low caste. In my earlier book, *Conscience and Coercion*, I described how a highly trained and prominent barrister in Karachi cleaned the bathroom in the guesthouse where we stayed. Were this outlook in social relations to take hold in the subcontinent, it would likely result in a cultural revolution.

What is striking about most of these Ahmadi associations is the synergism of a traditionalist piety that presupposes the reality and providential action of God and his revelation to the Promised Messiah and ongoing divine guidance of the khalifa, with a modern sense of organizational rationalization. Though much of the work of the youth organization is still done manually, including the book keeping and maintenance of the membership ledger, they do have a computerized desktop-publishing operation and as soon as the training is complete will no doubt move more fully into computerized operations.

The Khuddam headquarters contains registers of names and supplementary information on every member in Pakistan. I was shown a filing cabinet that contained the files of all the 950 chapters throughout the country. I wondered whether the scope and detail of the organizational structure threatened the achievement of the work for which the organization exists. This has happened in Protestant Christian organizations where so much energy is devoted to maintaining real estate and professional staff that what is ostensibly the main work of the church – evangelizing a broken and sinful humanity – is subordinated to the demands of institutional machinery. The Ahmadi youth organizations, however, are run almost totally with voluntary labour. Though there are thirty-two paid staff at the Pakistan national headquarters, the program is conducted mainly through the free and dedicated labour of members. The program is also funded by the one percent of income that all members donate. The contributions are still entered by hand in a large ledger book and receipts issued manually.

When I was offered tea in the Khuddam guesthouse my initial instinct was to refuse since it was Ramadan. The others, of course, were fasting. But the table had already been spread with cakes and cookies and a tea flask. I had established a warm rapport with the young men who were showing us about and so I appealed for their guidance in discovering an Islamic attitude and course of action. I explained how I had had a conversation a few days previously with someone in the street who had invited me into his house for tea. I had declined on the grounds that it was Ramadan but said that I would gladly return once the month of fasting had ended. I asked what the appropriate response should be in the face of their offer of tea. Was the Islamic thing to refuse it while others were fasting or to accept it because it was an expression of Islamic hospitality to the guest? The answer was that while most Muslims would no doubt take offence at anyone eating publicly during the month of fasting, the Ahmadis had a different attitude and in their eyes the proper thing for me to do was simply to accept the proffered tea. This I did but compromised by declining to eat any of the cakes and cookies.

Missionary Outreach

I returned one early morning from several fast turns around the compound grounds during which I met two other men walking briskly, and after bumping into each other twice, we carried on together. When they learned that I was the author of *Conscience and Coercion*, they were thrilled and shook my hand with great warmth and gratitude because the book has proved very useful to the *jama'at*, though I intended it basically as a more or less neutral exposition of Ahmadi faith and practice and of Ahmadi persecution in Pakistan. They were both returned missionaries, one from Indonesia and the other from Sri Lanka and Mauritius. The Ahmadis carry on extensive missionary work, particularly in West Africa where they are growing very rapidly but also throughout the Muslim world, creating, I gather, resentment on the part of Sunni Muslims who bridle at the apparent success of the Ahmadi missionary outreach.

The high degree of commitment required of missionaries, particularly in a former era, is displayed in the following accounts. Naseer, our guide, informed us that when he was posted as a missionary to Nigeria, he was separated for four years from his family. During that period he was unable to visit his family in Pakistan and they certainly were not able to go to Nigeria. There was a further separation when he was posted to England, where he was a missionary for four years before his family was able to join him. Munir, who supervises the Ahmadiyyat television studio on a voluntary basis for twelve hours a day, informed us that when he was posted to Nigeria, he spent three and one-half years without his family. When I pointed out to Naseer and Munir the sacrifice that this entailed, they compared their travails with those of an earlier generation of missionaries, some of whom endured twelve-year separations from their families in carrying out Ahmadi missionary work.

When I drew attention to the heroic dimension of this missionary sacrifice, Naseer replied that the Christian missionaries had done much the same. Many of them had, but some of the Christian missionaries lived more comfortable lives in the field than they did at home. Some of the missions with which we are acquainted in central India, Ratlam, Indore, and Mhow came with large bungalows and servants to clean, cook, wash the clothes, and attend to most of the physical mechanics of living. There was, of course, a price to be paid in the separation from home, friends, and family, but some of the missions certainly compensated their missionaries with pleasant lifestyles. This is not universally true; there were missions that demanded the lives not only of the missionaries but also of their spouses and children, who sometimes fell prey to disease.

Although we are not able to confirm this with specific numbers, we have the impression that the Ahmadi missionaries on the whole live rather abstemiously on restricted stipends, though the missionaries of today have it somewhat easier. As the movement grows and people become wealthier, the *jama'ats* have more money at their disposal while modern means of transportation make it feasible for families to fly to distant locations. Naseer reported that some of the early Ahmadi missionaries to West Africa went from East African ports across the Sahara at great risk because it was cheaper than taking a sailing ship around the Cape to the West African ports.

Another former missionary who had spent more than twenty years in Scandinavia and then almost two years in Zurich, Switzerland, brought to light various aspects of the Ahmadi missionary outreach. Projects abroad, particularly in West Africa and, in an earlier period, in East

Africa, seem to be funded largely by Pakistani Ahmadis, not by the Ahmadi diaspora. Another former missionary of our acquaintance had worked in Kenya and Tanzania for the largest part of his life, headquartered in Nairobi. The usual custom is for the *jama'ats* in the various countries to become self-supporting and so the contributions from a given country support the work of the movement in that country rather than abroad. The largest per capita donation of any country is Japanese, despite the small size of its Ahmadi community.

Hospital Outreach and Medical Practice

Peggy and I visited the Ahmadi Hospital one day in the congenial company of Naseer. We spent more than three hours touring all the departments of the hospital. As we passed through the gates into the courtyard we were confronted with a great deal of activity, none of it disorderly or confused, as patients and staff moved back and forth across the courtyard between the main hospital building and an adjacent out-patient building. Construction was going on to house new x-ray equipment, which was a gift from a doctor in the United States.

By far the majority of funding for the range of Ahmadi projects comes not, as we had supposed, from Ahmadis in the diaspora – Germany, the UK, Canada, the United States – who have done well and loyally remit a large part of their savings to the central community in Rabwah. Rather it is generated in Pakistan itself. There is a lot of wealth in Pakistan; it is simply very inequitably distributed. In spite of harassment and persecution, a significant group of Ahmadis continues to prosper financially, though it must be remembered that seventy to eighty percent of Ahmadis still live in villages and some of them are quite poor.

We were escorted down the long terrazzoed corridors to the administration offices where we met the hospital administrator, Colonel Muhammad Abdul-Khaliq, and Dr Latif Qureshi. A retired army man, Colonel Khaliq is a medical doctor who had resigned from the army when he had been refused promotion beyond his present rank because he is an Ahmadi. He had subsequently spent time in Sierra Leone as a missionary and had then been transferred to administer the hospital in Rabwah. Dr.

Qureshi had done his specialty in internal medicine and cardiology in the United Kingdom where he practised until he responded to the call to return to Rabwah and direct those departments in the Ahmadi Hospital.

We were served the customary tea and biscuits and *barfi*, the local fudgelike sweet of boiled milk and sugar, while we tried to set out the nature of our research, stressing that our interest was not so much in the doctrinal uniqueness of Ahmadiyyat as in Ahmadi social arrangements in the light of their revelation. Some of the points that were anticipated in our exchanges with Doctors Khaliq and Qureshi were later reiterated in greater detail to the head of gynaecology and obstetrics, Dr Nusrat Jahan, an effervescent woman who radiated competence and commitment.

We learned that over ninety percent of the patients served by the hospital are non-Ahmadis because the hospital caters to a wide surrounding geographical area. Non-Ahmadi Muslims and Christians come there with the confidence that they will be taken care of efficiently and lovingly. I asked what percentage of the hospital budget came from government funds and was told not a cent. The hospital is totally supported by Ahmadi funds, approximately sixty percent of which are generated by the fees that are charged and the other forty percent by donations from the Ahmadi community. Most of the contributions come from within Pakistan though some are sent from abroad. The Ahmadi donation is channelled to the hospital through the central council, or Anjuman, the governing or administrative authority of the Ahmadi movement, always, of course, under the supreme authority of the khalifa.

There are both men and women among the senior physicians, nurses, and back-up or support staff. The doctors meet in a mixed conference to discuss their cases and problems, though the women are veiled. Dr Qureshi told an amusing story about a female patient who said to him when she was unveiled for examination, "Do you recognize me?" to which he responded, "No." She had been one of his scrub nurses for four years and in spite of this sustained professional contact, Dr Qureshi had never seen her face and had not known who she was without her veil.

Dr Qureshi said that in the vast majority of cases there is no difficulty in his examining women patients. It is his practice, of course, to have a female nurse present but it is not the custom to have the husband or any other male protector present during the examination. It seems most patients readily understand the male doctor has a special role that ex=cuses him from the usual constraints of purdah upon the mingling of men and women. There have been some extreme cases of the sequestering of women in the practice of medicine amongst Muslims, but not in the Rabwah hospital. Naseer related the episode of the *hakim* (a doctor who specializes in herbal treatments) who, not being able to take the pulse of a female patient, would have the husband wrap a silk thread around the wrist, which would then be extended several yards to him. So sensitive was his touch that he would be able to feel the pulse beat along the silk thread. This does seem purdah carried to an extreme and I deem the story to be apocryphal.

In some Ahmadi meetings, in the local *jama'ats* or congregations, women may be present at the deliberations but must stay on the other side of a curtain. In the hospital the only restriction is that the women doctors be veiled. Male and female nurses train together, but the women must be veiled during classes. Female nurses always remain veiled, except when they are on women's surgical and medical wards where there are no male nurses. In the intensive care and cardiology units, which appeared to be well equipped with some of the latest equipment that is available in the West, we discovered that male and female nurses work together. In the ICU we talked with two young female nurses, aged nineteen and twenty-two, with long white gowns and veils, who were working alongside a male nurse. We were taken into the male surgical medical wings where the patients did not seem to object to being gawked at by a couple of foreigners. On the male wards the nurse attendants were male. On the female medical and surgical wards the attending nurses were all women. In almost every case I asked the female staff if they were married and learned to my surprise that a good number of them were. This immediately signalled that the conventional distinction between the public sphere, which belongs exclusively to the men, and the domestic sphere, which is the responsibility and vocation of women, is not rigidly observed.

Dr Nusrat had pursued her gynaecology and obstetrical specialty in the UK and had done very well. She could have had a successful and re-munerative practice either in the UK or the United States, to which she also received an invitation. She divorced when she concluded that her husband was not sufficiently committed to the truth of Ahmadiyyat and felt that she could not remain in a marriage with a disjunction of faith. As most Ahmadis do on any critical decision, she consulted with the khalifa, who advised her that she should give her services to the Rabwah hospital for a year on a trial basis. That was nine years ago. At the time a gynaecological unit did exist at the hospital but in embryonic form, and she has dedicated herself over the last nine years to the creation of what appears, to a lay observer like myself and to my Registered Nurse wife, to be a well-staffed, well-supplied, and efficient unit.

Dr Nusrat introduced us to the four women doctors, all obstetricians and gynaecologists, who work under her and to a number of the unit's nurses. They were all veiled because we men were present, but normally with only women in the unit they would remove their veils for ease and convenience. The veils do get in the way of speech. Dr Nusrat, who is a very enthusiastic and communicative person, was somewhat impeded in speaking to us through her veil.

Dr Nusrat reported that half of her female staff were married and that some had children but were managing to combine a public professional career with a domestic homemaker's role. It has to be recognized that theirs was a special case since their jobs required only minimal contact with men. Ahmadi Muslims are concerned not just that working women will be deflected from what they consider the divinely ordained women's sphere of homemaking, child-bearing, and child-rearing, but also that they will be mixing in an undesirable way with men who are not their husbands, fathers, or brothers. Work within the gynaecological and obstetrical units for the most part precludes such contact with males as could be deemed un-Islamic.

The obstetrics and gynaecology wing was well disciplined and immaculate. Dr Nusrat introduced us to patients, one of whom was a forty-year-old who after five miscarriages had finally brought a child to term. Dr Nusrat was preparing to perform a cesarean on her rather than run the risk of losing the baby.

We were taken into another cubicle where a woman was patiently waiting on the table for an ultrasound. Dr Nusrat, with some medical reservation, practises amniocentesis. This information precipitated a long discussion about abortion or other courses of action to be pursued when it is ascertained either by ultrasound or amniocentesis that grave foetal deformities exist. Like Dr Qureshi, Dr Nusrat held it to be consistent with Islamic principles to perform abortions to safeguard not only the life of the mother but her health as well where it would be gravely threatened by continuing a pregnancy. Cases involving the mother's health are more problematic and merge into the category of saving the mother's life. At first, it seemed that Dr Nusrat also believed that where prenatal diagnosis disclosed extreme deformity (e.g., if the foetus had no head), abortion was morally legitimate. After a certain amount of prodding, Dr Nusrat and Dr Qureshi testified that they would not withdraw treatment even in the case of an anencephalic baby (infants born without a brain). Dr Nusrat said that in her experience such babies rarely live so it becomes a nonissue, although she conceded the literature does report on cases that do survive and have treatment withdrawn, including nutrition and water, in order to bring about their death. This is a practice to which they would not subscribe. Their faith convinces them that ultimately God is the healer and that they are only the human agencies of the divine cure. There are cases that might seem from a medical point of view entirely hopeless but that are still open to special divine intervention should it be God's will. Accordingly, their practice is to fight to keep any infant alive as long as there are signs of life.

Candour demanded that we disclose that their view ran counter to that which Peggy and I hold, that in certain circumstances this unconditional preservation of life verges on inhumanity not just towards the suffering infant – if we can assume the presence of suffering in someone who does not have a cerebral cortex or consciousness – but also on the part of father, mother, and siblings. This is not to mention something that is usually discreetly avoided, namely the possible moral misuse of limited medical resources.

Dr Nusrat then ushered us into a delivery-room where a woman in the process of giving birth was being given oxygen. She turned her head to look at us, although just a moment before she had shown every sign of being in severe pain. Peggy went right inside to the table. I glanced at her but stood more discreetly in the doorway. Our visit to the hospital disclosed an eastern attitude among the patients of subordination to the authority of the learned and the professional and the assumption that if the authority figures have some reason for showing guests around, then the patients should simply accept it, which they appeared to do gladly.

Dr Nusrat runs both prenatal and postnatal training classes, not only for her staff of nurses and junior doctors but also for the patients. She has inaugurated and carried through an entire program from basic training to the effective delivery of complicated medical services. This she does with an ebullient commitment that is moving to behold. She talks unembarrassedly about her commitment to God, and of the legitimate spiritual authority of the Promised Messiah and his khalifa. She related the obligation of the hospital staff to radiate love to all their patients from wherever they came, in order to serve God. The fundamental motivation is the service of God through serving the needs of their patients. She shows her nursing staff a film called *The Inn of the Sixth Happiness*, which depicts a Christian missionary in China. She then editorializes to her staff, saying that if the Christian missionaries can give such sacrificial service, how much more so should Ahmadis, who live in the light of the revelation to the Promised Messiah.

As our tour of the hospital continued we removed our shoes, donned surgical gowns, masks, and caps, and inspected two operating theatres that were not then in use. These evinced a commitment to using the latest equipment provided by medical science that the community could possibly afford. The hospital is in a constant state of development. The architecture of the building shows the way section after section, wing after wing, have been added as funds become available. It has all been done in the face of the constitutional, legal, and practical hurdles that are put in the way of Ahmadi practice of their religion. Dr Nusrat seemed to be an exceptional person, enthusiastically literate and very expressive, highly competent and utterly committed to serving God as she feels it is demanded by the revelation made to the Promised Messiah. With people like that one can understand what appears to be the successful expansion of the missionary and humanitarian works of the movement.

Dr Qureshi said that the doctors at the Rabwah hospital find themselves dealing with very few psychological problems, although they are
fully aware of psychiatric medicine. They do occasionally confront schiz-
ophrenia but very few cases of depression. Suicide is extremely rare. In
his twenty-five years of practice he has encountered only two or three
cases. He ascribes the absence of depression and the relatively good mental health of his patients to the coherence and integrity of families. His
own view – shaped no doubt by ideological commitments – is that mental illness is usually a function of family breakdown. He construed family
disarray as largely a function of marital infidelity. When I speak of the
centrality of family in providing the sense of belongingness that minis-
ters to an endemic sense of aloneness, I typically think in terms of par-
ent-child relationships; Dr Qureshi focused instead on the destructive
consequences, as he viewed them, of conjugal infidelity. I raised the question how one could ever practise infidelity in this carefully segregated
society but he assured me that it is possible and that it happens.

In my own experience, mental and emotional problems are not so
much a result of tension and infidelity between spouses but of the damaging consequences of lovelessness and poor parental guidance and support of children. The palpably damaged personalities that I have encountered among my students over the years are the consequence of personal
alienation and rejection by parents. By the time people have reached
adulthood and entered married relationships, they are either relatively
invulnerable to further grave hurts or, alternatively, able to cope with
them and resolve the issues. So while I agreed with Dr Qureshi on the
centrality of the family in creating buoyant mental health and obviating
depression and darkness of soul, I differed in that I see the cause largely
in defective early parental-child relationships rather than in subsequent
conflicts – especially adulterous – between adults.

Education in Rabwah

I turn now to a visit that Peggy and I made to the Ahmadi school in
Rabwah. First a word of background. In 1972 the government of Pakistan

expropriated all the private schools that had been run by the Ahmadis at Rabwah. Other private educational institutions, mainly those run by Christians, were also expropriated. The result was a deterioration in the quality of education. We were told that some of the teachers in the state schools are disinclined to give solid instruction during the regular classes because they hope to recruit students for private tutoring after hours.

After observing the situation for a number of years, the Ahmadis in 1987 started a private school called the Nusrat Jahan Academy after the wife of the Promised Messiah. They took over a cluster of unplastered brick buildings on the outskirts of the town, behind the great Aksa Jumma Masjid, or Friday Mosque. These buildings had served as dormitories for the *Jalsa salana*, the annual convention that figures so prominently in Ahmadi practice. After the government of Pakistan forbade the *Jalsa*, the buildings lay empty. By no means refined, they are basically rows of low brick structures along lanes of beaten earth. The floors are concrete and since there are no windows natural light enters only by the doors that are left open. It is very chilly in the winter. During our visit in January and February the nighttime temperature hovered close to zero degrees on the coolest nights – these are not ideal learning conditions. Nevertheless the classes that we visited, and we must have visited ten of them, were cheerful and seemed to be functioning competently under adverse conditions. All the students and teachers, under their burqas, wore sweaters and jackets, and some even wore hats.

We began with the men's side of the school and interviewed the vice-principal, Thir Nasim. On his side of the school the boys were taught from the sixth grade up. From kindergarten, or preparatory, till grade five inclusive, the schooling is co-educational. That would take us up to about eleven years. From that point the sexes are divided with the boys continuing from the sixth until the tenth class on one side of the compound and the girls on the other, along with the junior school of kindergarten to five. As with male and female nurses in the hospital, there is some interaction among teachers of both sexes at school, although for the most part they function on separate sides of the school compound. We were later told that Hazoor had recently requested that where male teachers were not available, the women teachers should move over to the boys' school.

This must be recognized as a purely subjective impression, but one got the sense that the greatest energy and enterprise were being shown on the womens' side of the school. This prompts a reflection that we will explore further, that gender segregation, creating as it does different spheres of power, allows the women to run their own show without interference from the men. I am reminded of a situation I found myself in when I was a pastor assigned to my first full-time congregation, the All Peoples' Mission of the United Church of Canada, which had been run until my arrival by the Women's Missionary Society. Many of these women were competent well-educated women who for one reason or another had not married and had dedicated their lives and their professions to the service of the Church in evangelism, hospitals, schools, and social work. By 1956 the Women's Missionary Society had been assimilated into the regular courts of the Church, and thus came under the authority of the Presbytery, a body that at the time was largely dominated by men. In fact the women missionaries, in a curious turn of phrase, referred to the Presbytery as "the men." This was not said pejoratively but often with an undercurrent of sadness, if not resentment that the autonomy that they had once enjoyed had now been relegated to the authority of the men in the Presbytery. Segregation had worked well for the Women's Missionary Society, at least in terms of autonomous, self-directed judgments and activities.

Of the forty-six teachers at the school on the women's side, twenty were married. Of those, we assumed that the majority had children. They viewed with alarm and perhaps disgust the idea of having children tended by daycare centres, relying instead as they do on family members, relatives, and "babysitters," meaning the age-old tradition, amongst the socioeconomic classes that can afford it, of having an *ayah*, or servant who assists in the raising of the children. One must recall that servants in the subcontinent come very cheap.

We had difficulty getting a consistent fix on the community's attitude towards Ahmadi women working outside the home. Peggy had earlier got the impression at Lejna (the women's organization) that the ideal certainly is the stay-at-home wife, giving herself single-mindedly to the creation of a good home and to the child-bearing and child-rearing function. Whatever time she has beyond this would be dedicated to volunteer work on behalf of the movement, typically through Lejna. Clearly, however, a number of the women both in the hospital and at the school were managing to combine professional career and homemaking. They claim (perhaps naturally enough) that there is no contradiction between their participation in the public sphere of medicine and education and their commitment to the domestic and child-rearing role. It may be that this reconciliation is possible in a humanly non-damaging way only because of their ability to rely on a strong family support system.

The Ahmadi school is a private school that requires that the students pay fees. Up to grade ten the fees are 165 rupees (approximately eight dollars Canadian in 1995) per month and in what they call the intermediate school, which has yet to receive its first students from the lower grades, the fees will be 250 rupees (fourteen dollars Canadian) per month. There are two streams in the boy's section of the school, Urdu and English. The Urdu stream takes English seventy minutes daily as a separate subject and the English stream studies Urdu as a subject. Students in both streams receive religious instruction of two sorts. One is the required textbook stipulated by the government of Pakistan, which is basically a course in Islamic studies. I asked whether it contained any anti-Ahmadi assertions, to which the staff replied "Not yet, but with revisions of the textbooks, the Ahmadi will eventually come under explicit censure in the textbooks which they will be required to teach." In addition to this there is specific instruction in Ahmadi doctrine and practice, for which there is no textbook, only the general religious understanding of the teachers, all of whom are Ahmadi.

The boy's section contains 240 students from grade six to ten, and on the girl's side there were 832 boys and girls together, that is, the young boys until grade five and the girls up to grade five and beyond, totalling over a thousand students in the school.

There are four periods of religious instruction per week. Three for Islamayat (the prescribed government syllabus) and one for Ahmadiyyat, which is specifically Ahmadi instruction.

The men served us tea and *barfi*, the customary Pakistani sweet, but the women, who also offered us tea, were much more thorough in introducing us to their school. They took us from classroom to classroom, in most of which Peggy and I said a few words to the students of encouragement and appreciation of their work. The students are invariably courteous in a way that I believe we were in the Ontario public school system some fifty to sixty years ago. As we entered the classroom they all came to their feet immediately and said, "Good Morning, Sir" and remained standing until invited to sit down. They wear a kind of school uniform, a maroon sweater and grey scarf, and all have an appearance of seriousness and industriousness. The teachers, of course, were all veiled. They spoke English with varying degrees of fluency but their instruction is all in English – there is no Urdu stream on the girls' side. The female teachers feel that English-medium instruction is the way to ensure excellence for their students in the modern world, though they acknowledge that "they [the men on the other side of the school] don't agree with us; they don't see it as we do." Their expectation is that as the present group of Urdu-medium students on the men's side works its way through the system, even that side will follow exclusively English-medium instruction as the present students from kindergarten to grade five move over to the boy's school.

It was interesting that one of the teachers who had shown us around her part of the school with such enthusiasm, with her veil which she had to hike up with her fingers slipping down past her nose from time to time as she continued her exposition of the activities of the school, was unable even to come forward to meet me when we went to her brother's house for tea on a subsequent occasion. Peggy, of course, visited with her at some length in the ladies' part of the house but I was diverted quickly off to Anas Ahmad's study. The woman with whom I had spent an hour, in the company of several other people, was totally absent from the exchange on philosophical matters with her brother.

We toured every classroom on the girls' side from kindergarten up to grade seven, which is as high as they go at the present time as the students move upward through the system. In every class we directed a few questions to the teachers regarding the subjects they were teaching, be it the English language, mathematics and physics, or Urdu and Persian. Persian and Arabic are compulsory subjects in the elementary school; after grade five students can choose one or the other. In viewing this school it is easy to understand why the literacy rate is almost one hundred percent amongst Ahmadis. They put high stress on the importance of being able to read the Holy Books and this, of course, spills over into a public career where education provides competency and power. In fact one of the slogans painted on the wall of one of the brick classrooms was "Knowledge is Power."

There is a single blackboard across the front of each classroom, in line with the open door to provide natural light. There seemed to be very few pedagogical tools.

The students from poorer families who are unable to pay the fees are subsidized by the *jama'at*, that is to say, by the Anjuman, or central council, out of Ahmadi central office funds. There are a few non-Ahmadi students but not many: the Ahmadis feel a primary obligation to educate their own group, and some non-Ahmadis are reluctant to pay the fees, preferring the free education offered at the state school, inadequate as that education may be. Those non-Ahmadis who seek education in the Ahmadi school will be accommodated.

We were at the school for two hours and saw ample evidence of the special dedication of the Ahmadis to a well-rounded program for their devotees. One of the reasons why the Sunnis have severely condemned the Ahmadis is their alleged exclusiveness; Ahmadis are quite convinced that Ahmadiyyat represents the true Islam and that non-Ahmadis are incomplete or inadequate Muslims; hence their rigorous missionary program. This echoes a certain kind of Protestant fundamentalism, perhaps especially Pentecostalism, which feels that mainline Christians remain unsaved and are therefore appropriate targets for those who want them to be born again and incorporated into the true Christian faith and fellowship, that is, their own brand of fundamentalist Christianity.

THEOLOGICAL TRAINING

On our visit to the Jammia Ahmadiyya, or Theological Training School, we were greeted cordially by the principal, Syed Mahmud Ahmad, usually simply called Nasir, whom we remembered very well from our visit in 1987. We had established a special rapport then, partly because we both shared a passion for hill walking and trekking. Because these buildings tend to be damp and chilly in the winter, the principal was seated outside in the sun, at a small table in the driveway, which was distinctly more comfortable.

After introductions to some of the staff, including Muhammad Ali whom we came to know well, we proceeded to the great hall where approximately 250 students, the full complement of the school, aged roughly seventeen to twenty-three, were assembled to hear a lecture that I had been invited to give only about three-quarters of an hour earlier. In typically courteous Pakistani style, they rose to their feet as we came in and remained standing until invited to resume their seats. The principal introduced me in the customary generous way and then I began a presentation on the nature of my present research project in Rabwah on the tension between, and possible reconciliation of, tradition and modernity. I sought to contextualize my interest in researching this community by drawing attention to the diversity in approach to religious studies between the secular university in which I teach, with its emphasis on phenomenology and presumptively neutral or objective study of the religious data, and that of the seminary, on the other hand, which is the Western model for the kind of Ahmadi institution we were visiting. My explanation of the contemporary conflict between traditional and modern world views and value systems allowed me to explicate the way many of us in the West understand religion as participation in symbolic materials such as rituals, doctrines, and moral practices that mediate an understanding of reality and commensurate values.

After the lecture we adjourned to the driveway outside the main doors, where we were served tea and cookies in a gloriously warm sun. We carried on some of the discussion that had been precipitated by my lecture and introduced new themes like the proper way to discuss and translate terms like Allah in the Qur'an, and the proper translation of the first sura in the Italian version of the Qur'an. We then moved to a magnificent rose garden, still producing, in January weather, marvellous roses in assorted hues of red, white, and yellow. The garden was adjacent to a small mosque that served the students of the college. Beyond that was one of the main hostels in which students are accommodated, and the common kitchens and dining-rooms where they take their food. Beyond that rise the stark and dry rock outcroppings that are characteristic of Rabwah, surmounted nowadays by a telecommunications tower. The students used to have a climbing competition to see who could reach the summit quickest but this is now forbidden because a magistrate with a house nearby took it upon himself to prevent access to the mountain. I had wondered whether I would, before I left the place, climb it, and although the inclination to tackle high places is receding I might have attempted it had I not found that it was now forbidden. (In the end I climbed the steep west face twice – the first time with a young missionary and again when Peggy and I made an early-morning ascent up a more difficult route by ourselves.) We took a very cordial leave from the principal and his colleagues with an invitation to return to his home for dinner.

DORMANT COLLEGES

Down the street from our bungalow's Rose Garden are two grand-looking buildings, a boys' college and a girls' college. College in this context means education that is pursued beyond grade ten which the Ahmadis regard as accreditation year. The first two years of college give the successful student a FA or FSc – a Faculty of Arts or a Faculty of Science Certificate. It is also called intermediate school. A further two years leads to exams that are set by the University of Punjab with which the colleges are affiliated. Successful completion of the second two years results in a BA or a BSc degree. Beyond this, there is presently a MA in Arabic at the girls' college and previously there was an MSc in physics at the boys' college.

These colleges at one time were administered by the Ahmadis. They built, funded, and administered them with only the most marginal contribution from the state even though more than half of the students from the surrounding areas were non-Ahmadis. These Ahmadi colleges had high educational standards, and the top performers at the University of Punjab exams were typically found to be students from Rabwah. These colleges were taken over by the state in 1973 under Bhutto's nationalization scheme. The extensive properties and buildings were simply expropriated without any compensation whatsoever. After 1974, the government began to transfer Ahmadi staff from the Rabwah schools to outside areas; even though there had always been non-Ahmadis instructors on the staff, the majority had been Ahmadi teachers. This ratio now tilted in favour of non-Ahmadi instructors. Again, nationalization of schools affected not only the Ahmadis but also other religious bodies such as Christian churches that ran educational institutions. Some time later the state bank recommended to the government of Pakistan the return of these private institutions because of the great cost to the government of running them. Monsoor Khan believes that some of them were in fact returned to Christian institutions. But he also believes that even if a general program of restoration were to be carried through, the Ahmadis would be the last to receive their schools back.

These Ahmadi colleges were in some ways elite institutions, though they were not restricted to the upper and middle classes: Monsoor Khan took great pains to point out that they accepted students from all classes. Fees were waived in the case of poor students in order to allow universal access to the educational system.

Theology was also taught in the period of Ahmadi control. It was compulsory for the Ahmadi students and optional for the non-Ahmadis. There were obligatory prayers in the afternoon for all students. The non-Ahmadis could if they wish separate and pray under their own imam, or prayer leader. Since the government takeover of these schools, the common perception is that their educational level has decreased severely. A large property on the outskirts of Rabwah holds a partially completed building that was to accommodate the new master's program in physics for the boys' college and now remains unoccupied.

Qaza (Communal Court)

On one busy day I visited the Qaza, the Ahmadi judicial board. In *Conscience and Coercion*, I misleadingly referred to the Qaza as a shari'a court. The Ahmadis objected to the term shari'a because there is a Pakistan government court of that description and they did not want the government to think that the Ahmadis were trying to run a parallel judicial system – the Ahmadis already have sufficient problems. I had an interview first with Idris, amir of Lahore district, who is also a lawyer and a member of the Qaza board. We sat in on a trial. Across one side of the table there were five Ahmadi judges. Two of them were civil lawyers and therefore versed in the Pakistani civil law, and three were respected members of the *jama'at*, trained in *fiqh*, or Islamic jurisprudence. The jury could thus not only adjudicate matters of Islamic law and those pertaining to civil law but it could also deal with any conflicts that might emerge between the two systems of law.

The case in point dealt with the redistribution of a marriage dowry; a woman from a very wealthy and highly regarded family felt she had married beneath her class and wanted now to be released from the marriage, claiming that she was being ill used. Moreover, she wanted to recover some of the investment that she had brought to that marriage. The husband's family, on the other hand, wanted the wife back and insisted that as they had treated her well she was not entitled to recover part of her dowry if she chose to leave the marriage. This was going on in Urdu while Idris and I sat very close to the table, perhaps a bit rudely I thought, but nobody seemed to pay any attention to us nor to Idris's running commentary in English explaining the procedures to me.

I was then taken to the office of the president of the Qaza board. During a long, cordial, and intense interview, I asked a number of questions and provoked considerable discussion on the intention of the Qaza board. It is a fascinating institution intended to adjudicate conflicts within the Ahmadi community. Its ultimate sanction is a moral sanction; members of the *jama'at* who mutually subscribe to the Ahmadi tradition and its prohibitions and prescriptions generally agree to abide by the findings of this court. It handles only civil cases, not criminal cases. By civil I mean problems such as those relating to marriage, divorce, money matters, property conflicts, ownership, right of way, and contracts.

There are four and perhaps five levels of adjudication. The first is a hearing before a single judge who is recruited from a panel of about thirty Qaza judges. If either the plaintiff or the defendant is displeased with the verdict, he or she can appeal to the next level, where the case is heard before two judges. The appeals can escalate to another level where there are three judges and then to the final judicial level of appeal, the one I sat in on, which comprises five judges. From its judgment there is no right of appeal. This does not preclude a dissatisfied litigant from making a direct appeal to the khalifa in London, where at the very least the litigant is allowed to vent his displeasure at the verdict and testify to his sense of not being dealt with justly. This is not a right but rather a last personal attempt to receive vindication from the khalifa.

The president of the Qaza board reported that 99.5 percent of cases are satisfactorily settled and do not entail any appeal to the khalifa, who hears perhaps three or four such special complaints every year. The court handles about thirty cases per month. In 1994 they handled in total 257 cases. Ninety-nine percent of the defendants appear to respond to charges. They are not obliged legally to appear but their voluntary commitment of faith to Ahmadi practice and discipline means that nearly all will respond to an appeal by the Qaza to reply before the board to the charges of the plaintiffs. If they do not appear they are subjected to a discipline, which paradoxically consists of the refusal to accept their donations to the *jama'at*. This is considered a severe penalty within the Ahmadi communal system because it deprives the refused person of a sense of full participation in the community. The ultimate sanction if a person refuses to submit to the authority of the court can be tantamount to an excommunication whereby the khalifa, in writing, will simply say, "I discharge you from your *bai'at*," the pledge of allegiance to the khalifa, which is the criterion of adult membership in the Ahmadi movement.

The president ascribed the high rate of success in reaching settlements not only to the shared values and commitments of the litigants but also because they find that most disputes are not about the facts, which can usually be objectively ascertained, but about interpretation. Their experience is that the people who come before the court have genuinely sincere views about what is really the case, and the judicial process serves to clarify their understanding and therefore alter their conviction about the correctness of their position.

The Ahmadi court also strives to achieve reconciliation of the parties so that the result is not only a judicial settlement but also a growing together of previously alienated disputants within the community.

The advantages of the court are great, besides maintaining the unity of the community. It saves an enormous outlay of money for people involved in a civil dispute as well as huge amounts of energy and time. These Ahmadi lawyers and judges give their time voluntarily. The president, for example, is a prominent Lahore lawyer who comes down once a week or once a fortnight to preside over a jury. As with all the Qaza judges, his time and expertise are given as a free service to God and the *jama'at*.

He told me of his sister, who brought a charge against a non-Ahmadi in a civil court in 1977. The case is only now going to the court of appeal. This despite a degree of special treatment – as a lawyer the president was able to exert pressure on friends within the court to accelerate her case. It can take twenty-five to thirty years typically for a case to work its way through the Pakistani legal system to the provincial courts of appeal. Partly in recognition of this lamentable state of affairs, the second khalifa established the Ahmadi court. The intention of the present khalifa is that all cases should be settled within six months. This the court finds sometimes too optimistic, but it strives to have disputes resolved within one year.

When I went out for my morning walk at 6:30 A.M., already there was a slight rose-coloured tinge to the sky to the east, although the moon was still bright in the west. I joined forces with the *hakim* (herbal doctor) that I had met in the Gol Bazaar on my first or second day here. He was going counterclockwise, while I always go clockwise. Whenever I have met walkers, they also are going counterclockwise in emulation, I believe, of the circumambulation of the Ka'ba, the cube-shaped building that is the focal point of the Muslim *hajj*, or pilgrimage, in Mecca. The counterclockwise circumambulation is intended to keep the heart side of the body closest to the Ka'ba. I was walking, as I thought, fairly swiftly but he set a blistering pace. He had worked in the office of the private secretary to Hazoor in London after 1984 when Hazoor fled there from Pakistan. He had learned the art of speed walking from Hazoor, who walked four or five kilometres daily at a rapid pace. He told me that he was sixty-five years of age and warmly shook my hand when I told him that I was sixty-four. But I went back to Peggy like a beaten dog with my tail between legs and I had to confess how hard I was breathing in trying to keep up with his very fast stride.

Peggy communicated to Sharif, our bearer, her requirement of help to prepare her Italian spaghetti dinner for eight members of the staff of Tehrik-i-jadeed who had been especially helpful to us during the past months. She had some difficulty locating all the appropriate ingredients so it was only an improvised facsimile of the real thing, but the dinner went off very well.

I had been plagued by a chronic unsatisfactoriness or discontent for which it was hard to ascribe the cause. Some of it was due to disappointment that we were not going to make it back up to the mountains, partly because of the decreased initiative of encroaching age but also because of warnings that the country was coming apart. Even in the Swat valley where we had been planning to go, there were killings as a result of sectarian strife. Karachi was ablaze and rocked by severe violence, dramatized by the killing of two American diplomats and the wounding of a third as their van stopped at a light in Karachi.

I do not think I have ever dreamed so vividly as I did in Pakistan. I do not know why – perhaps it was the religious cultural context. As I noted earlier, the Ahmadis believe very strongly in the revelatory power of dreams and rely on their deliverances for guidance in everyday life. The dreams of the Promised Messiah and of the khalifa are pivotal in shaping the life and decisions of the community, but the lives of ordinary devotees are also guided by their own personal dreams.

Gender

part two
GENDER

LEFT: Eid prayers in Rabwah showing the
women's section separated from the
men's by a colourful wall of drapes

RIGHT: After numerous miscarriages,
this glowing new mother of roughly forty
holds her newborn son. Peggy gave each
of them gifts she brought from Canada

LEFT: Peggy with some of the children
who attend the 100 Houses school

MIDDLE: Peggy with her friend
Dr Nusrat Jahan, director of the
Obstetrics-Gynaecology unit at the
Fazel Amar Hospital in Rabwah

RIGHT: Two young nurses
from Rabwah Hospital who
assisted at the eye clinic

LEFT: This friend is a poetess, a director of Lejna, and wife of Mirzah Ghulam Ahmad

RIGHT: Peggy was invited into the bridal chamber to meet this young Rabwah bride. We sat on the bridal bed, the decorating of which with garlands, ribbons, and beads is given great importance. The bride scarcely communicated, perhaps exhausted by the three-day prewedding preparations of her face, hair, hands, and feet

CHAPTER FOUR

Purdah and Vocation

Peggy and I went for a walk down some of the minor roads of Rabwah, westward towards the outskirts of the town, and came upon a commotion down one of the side streets. Making our way to its source, we found that we were involved in the second part of the three-part wedding ritual. We were invited into the *shamianas*, the big marquees, Peggy on one side of the road in the women's section and I on the other side in the men's section. Folding chairs had been set up auditorium style, focused on the central part of the marquee where there was an open square against the back of which sat the groom, a vigorous and handsome figure flanked by various brothers, fathers and relatives, and the preacher who had given the *khutba* the last two times that I was at the *jumma* prayer. This was a simple ritual marked by the customary reading from the Qur'an, then readings from the Durri thamin, the collected devotional poetry of the Founder, then a further recitation from the Qur'an followed by the imam's sermon delivered without notes in a simple conversational style.

This was followed by silent prayer with the hands upraised before the face in the customary Ahmadi style. We have observed how often Ahmadis have recourse to silent prayer. The other evening when we went to the rock-climbing school at the Chenab River just at the *maghreb* prayer time, silence was quietly called for and the assembled gathering of students, instructors, climbers, teachers, and onlookers simply raised their hands before their faces, heads slightly inclined, eyes closed, most of them facing towards the sunset, and prayed silently. This was not the ritual *salat*, but we might call it a congregational silent prayer.

The first part of the wedding ritual is the *nika*, which is basically a legal-social contract, or covenant, between the two families. The *nika* must also be signed by the bride or by her surrogate or guardian, indicating her consent to the marriage. The second part of the ritual, which follows on another day, is the gathering that Peggy and I happened upon – an invocation of blessing as the bride and groom see each other for the first time: the groom has never laid eyes on the bride and the bride has seen only a photograph of the groom. Peggy on the woman's side reported to me later that the bride was a very beautiful woman. Following the prayer and blessing ceremony, the groom crosses the street and secures his bride, whom he then escorts to his home where they will spend the first conjugal night together in a festally decorated bridal chamber. The next day, the *wallima* will take place, a merry communal dinner celebrating the consummation of the marriage. It is assumed (with whatever proofs other than a declaration we do not know) that the marriage has been sexually consummated and is therefore constituted a complete union calling forth the *wallima* celebration. Peggy and I were picked up around two o'clock and driven to the *wallima* dinner, which also took place within a large *shamiana*. I have to confess to welcoming the occasion not only for its religious and anthropological value but also for a change in our rather austere diet.

Street Scenes

On a mid-morning, Peggy and I left our books and papers on the brick patio adjacent to our guesthouse and strolled into the shopping area of the town. It was remarkably busy, perhaps because of the closing of the shops for the midday congregational prayer on the preceding Friday. All the market stalls were in full swing, the shops were open, and crowds were bustling in the street.

The most striking feature for the foreigner is the women in complete purdah. The most prevalent garb is the black long overcoat-type burqa and head covering to which is added a veil across the lower part of the eyes, the nose, and the mouth. This is consistent with the heightened conservatism of the Ahmadis, who probably take the Qur'anic injunction of modesty and segregation of women to a further extent than most Sunni Muslims in Pakistan. We have even seen a few of the Afghan-style burqas that cover the woman from the crown of her head to the ground with only a little latticework at the eyes permitting reduced visibility.

While Peggy was inside buying a pair of plastic flip-flops to wear into the shower, I stood in the street and watched the passers-by. One woman who looked small and rather young, accompanied by a man of between thirty-five and forty, presumably her husband, who strode ahead of her, craned her head to look at me standing there in the street. It was curious to see this hooded head swing close to 180 degrees to stare at me even as she walked forward and past me. I thought, fortunately her husband is walking ahead and has not seen this little drama. Perhaps she was a sister and not a wife, though typically that would only partially mitigate her action. Most women, but by no means all, do avert their gaze and cast their eyes downward, but some maintain a steady and unembarassed regard. I suspect that it only applies to foreigners.

On another excursion to the main shopping street Peggy entered the shoestore while I remained standing in the street. Two Ahmadi women fully veiled and in burqa went past me and into the shop. They began an immediate conversation with Peggy and I felt that I should not enter right away. One of them was to be married in Toronto at the end of February and her English was quite good. Unlike Muslim women in general and Ahmadi women in particular, they were not the least bit shy in carrying on a conversation in front of me once I had entered the shop. When I drew this to our friend Naseer's attention, he said that they must have been from abroad and indeed it turned out that one of them had recently returned from Germany. Naseer thought that their much greater openness and willingness to engage in conversation with a strange man, even though accompanied by his wife, was a legacy of their foreign sojourn.

Anas Ahmad expressed a view that puts Islam on the side of relative liberality in the question of purdah, or segregation of the sexes. He enunciated a mediating view that insists on the primacy of certain fundamental principles of separation between the sexes, while at the same time affirming the historical relativity of particular ways of embodying this separation, including forms of dress.

He said that the fundamental demand of Islam is that social mixing of men and women be avoided because it threatens social harmony. He alluded to the Hadith in which the Prophet Muhammad says there are two sources of damage to Islam: the first is money and the second is women. Moroccan sociologist Fatima Mernissi describes this as the Muslim fear of an active "female sexuality." If it is not restrained (by the institution of veiling for example) it will lead to social chaos, or *fitna* (Mernissi, *Beyond the Veil*, 41–5). That being the case, it is necessary that men and women be allowed contact only in the most carefully guarded ways. As I left Anas, I put on the agenda for our next discussion the reasons for this terror of social mixing, as I called it perhaps unflatteringly – though the prohibition upon what was typically described as free social mixing was universally held. I suspect that the cause is to be seen in the Islamic perception that men, without rigorous social restraints – which are divinely inspired ultimately – would give way to unbridled sexual lust and rapacity. Moreover, one detects some uneasiness at the latent sexual aggression of women, which has to be carefully restrained lest it corrupt society and destroy cordial social relations. Some scholars have noted that, unlike the Christian tradition, which typically conceives of women as passive sexual beings, the Muslim view grants women some sexual rights (a husband's failure to perform sexually, for example, is one of the few grounds on which a wife can initiate divorce), but it then restrains these rights out of fear of social chaos.

For the moment let us simply note that in Anas Ahmad's view, particular forms of embodying the separation of the sexes, especially the veil, are not seen as absolute and universally binding. In the Pakistani cultural context, the Ahmadis generally view the veil as obligatory and I don't think we have ever been in a society, apart from Afghanistan, in which the veil was so widely used. Most of the women on the street have a long dark burqa, a black head-covering (abri), and then a black veil, which must hang in such a way that the slope of the woman's breast is also hidden. But what is appropriate for a Pakistani culture is not, in Anas's view, mandatory for other cultures. The Lejna women have told Peggy that they do not expect European or North American converts to Ahmadi Islam to take up the veil. This more liberal view tends to reconcile an absolute revealed principle in the Qur'an with the necessity of applying it in historically and culturally relative ways. We noted that even within Pakistani society, the question of the veil is also made relative according to social class. The servant girl who brought us our food and tea was not veiled. When I observed that she was without a veil, Anas said that it depended on the social class. This would be consistent with Leila Ahmed's analysis of the practice of veiling in *Women and Gender in Islam*. She argues that, following the practice among Greeks, Romans, and Jews, veiling in the early Muslim community was connected to social status. The prophet's wives were the first to adopt the veil and practise seclusion to distinguish themselves from other members of the community. In other words, there appears to be a kind of classism with respect to purdah whereby the higher a woman's social elevation, the higher her degree of hiddenness. As is customary during my visits, I never saw any of the women in the household, except as shadowy images looking down the hallway just to see what kind of husband Peggy, with whom they had been visiting, might have.

During Peggy's many visits with the women of Rabwah the obvious question was raised: When does a young girl adopt purdah? Peggy assumed that it was instituted when a girl began her menses, but in fact this was not the case. Purdah is embraced as soon as a young girl develops a bustline, whether that predates or follows menses. Several mothers assured Peggy that often a daughter will beg to wear a burqa prematurely. It is worn as a proud badge of maturity and also serves as protection from the gaze of young men.

Legitimate Vocational Spheres and Social Mixing

One day in Lahore Peggy and I sat on chairs on the lawn of the courtyard alongside the Ahmadi Masjid on a lovely and warm late January day, the blue sky aflutter with at least a dozen kites. Kite flying seems to be a specialty of the children in Lahore, particularly as spring draws near. We had just come from a long and useful exchange in the deputy amir's office of the Dar-al-Zikr, or place of worship, since the Ahmadis are not allowed by law to call their places of worship a mosque or masjid.

We spoke with Major Latif and Ijaz, the two deputy amirs of the *jama'at* in Lahore and also with General Naseer Ahmad, a major general now retired. In the context of explicating my research on Ahmadis as a case study of the tension between tradition and modernity, I said that we were focusing on the gender and family issue as a point of entry into this conflict of ethos. Peggy asked some specific questions about gender, which permitted Ijaz to enunciate his understanding of the Ahmadi position. He said, in short, that there is a women's sphere and a men's sphere, and that these spheres (although he did not say so at that point) are determined by the ontological difference in the creator's intention in making men and women. In addition, there is a community sphere in which there is some limited mixing between men and women. Our interlocutors agreed that the distinctiveness of women and the necessity of purdah do not require the abolition of women from the professions: their own children were cases in point. The general's son is a PhD in aeronautical and mechanical engineering, presently at the State University of Virginia, and his daughter is teaching in a medical institution in Stockton, California. Major Latif's niece, who is presently in Scarborough, Ontario, is a five-medal winner from the All Women's Medical College in Lahore.

Ijaz pointed out that in the consultative meetings, or *shuras*, women take part in the discussions and consultations. They do, but the consultations with women take place either in the gallery or behind curtains. Peggy asked how long the Ahmadi community would be able to maintain its rather strict version of purdah given that an increasing number of

Pakistani women, no doubt under the pressure of exposure to Western media, particularly films and television, are relinquishing the veil.

Ijaz replied that the question from their point of view is not how long the Ahmadi policy of segregation would last but how long the secular world could last in light of the increasing disarray of social and family life in the West. The West's push for freedom is a law of diminishing returns as can be seen, in the Ahmadi perception, in the increase of family breakdown and the spread of AIDS.

In response to their view that the *shura* is evidence of the Ahmadi Muslim acceptance of public vocations for women, Peggy pointed out that one could construe the *shura* as engagement in the public sphere, just as one could so construe the sight of veiled nurses and male nurses working side by side in the Rabwah hospital. What appears to be proscribed is what they call social mixing, which proscription is based on Qur'anic injunctioned boundaries set by Allah. The point of Peggy's interjection was that one cannot overwork the participation of women in the *shura* consultations because this would fit within the narrow category of public work which is acceptable on Ahmadi Muslim principles, although certainly not widely practised as yet.

Major Latif then broke in with an attempt to clarify what was objectionable from the point of view of Ahmadi Muslim convictions. "No free mixing is permissible," he declared and then he defined this basically as what we would call dating, although he would not use that term – mainly a boy and a girl going off alone together to the cinema. Ijaz pointed out that this would be taken as circumstantial evidence of indiscreet dealings between the boy and the girl. The way he put it is that if there is a chance of slipping, it must be avoided. But again, this begs the question what is it that they are terrified of in prohibiting this social mixing. Now we had a move towards an answer. The social mixing is, in Roman Catholic nomenclature, an occasion to sin so that one must be diligent in avoiding not only sin but, if one is wise and prudent, also the circumstances that allow sin to arise. In Ijaz's terms one should not give Satan a chance. Although we do not approve of this position (which is beside the point in any case given the phenomenological nature of our research), we insisted that we understood the desire to restrict the free mixing of girls and boys in the form of unchaperoned dating, from within their premises.

Peggy pointed out that she was allowed to be present for what must have been close to a three-hour discussion whereas the wives of our interlocutors were not. Such discussions, they asserted, could take place but it would be amongst the women, not in the presence of men who are beyond the permissible boundaries, that is to say, men to whom they are not related as father, husband, brother, or uncle. They added that Peggy was present out of respect for Nino because Nino allowed it. It was not clear why they would not similarly allow their wives to take part in the same kind of discussion. To keep the issue clear, I suggested that we restrict our purview to encounters amongst married couples with both spouses present. We pointed out that when we went to Anas Ahmad's home, Peggy was immediately ushered into the women's meeting-room towards the rear and I was isolated with Anas in his book-lined study. Similarly when we went to the home of the principal of the Jammia, Peggy again was immediately met and escorted to another section of the house where she carried on her conversations and had her dinner with the women.

Peggy heightened the nature of the question by pointing out that I, in company with Peggy and Naseer, had already spent an hour with Anas's sister at the school as she, in her burqa and, admittedly, behind her veil, had escorted us from classroom to classroom and answered all our questions about the nature of the education that the Ahmadis give their young people in Rabwah. In spite of that meeting, when we went to her home she was not able to greet me again. We could not avoid the inference that there was a little bit of fudging going on here. Peggy conceded, as did I, that the proscription on "free mixing," or dating, among young people is intelligible. Our immediate question, however, was why there was no social mixing, even of a sober and refined kind, among mature married couples. On this there was no clear answer apart from reliance on apodictic revelation.

On the question of dress, they pointed out that purdah does not necessarily mean the burqa and the veil. They revealed that the present dress is actually more extreme than it was in the time of the Prophet when female attire would have been more relaxed. The present strictures are seen as an accommodation to subcontinental culture, where given the "dirty social environment," by which is meant the prevalence of loose and rapacious conduct, a woman would be susceptible to male predations were she unprotected by the concealments of the veil and the burqa. They pointed out that the heavy covering that is widely adopted now is, in fact, a Muslim appropriation from Hindu rajput culture. There is recognition of the culturally determined elements that insinuate themselves into the whole institution of purdah.

Variations in Purdah

Two interesting exchanges took place on the question of purdah. While driving up to Pindi with Mujeeb-ur-Rhaman and Hamid, I observed how skewed our impressions of purdah would have been had we restricted our data only to the Rabwah experience, which is a highly conservative enclave of Ahmadis, where the almost uniform garb is a full burqa, headscarf, and veil across the lower part of the face.

We had spent the previous evening at the home of the young doctor Alim and his wife Falak. We were quite astonished to see that she received us unveiled. Though she did have on a headscarf, her face was totally uncovered. When we arrived at the door Peggy was motioned forward to where Falak was standing at the end of the hall and I had assumed that we men, Alim and I, would turn left into another room that was just off the entrance way; instead Alim motioned me forward. We remarked how pleasantly surprised we were by this change in social arrangements. Their understanding of purdah was that it is basically fidelity to the principle and value of feminine modesty and decorum and the correlative male respect and chivalry. This does not in itself mandate any particular form of dress, although there are modest limits beyond which one cannot go.

Alim and Falak believed that they had Hazoor on their side. They described the criticism that Hazoor had received from some of the conservatives in Rabwah when he had appeared on television conducting a question-and-answer period with women seated in the audience before him without hijab. To which criticism Hazoor had replied that he was not a tailor to make veils and headscarves on the spot for women. On this understanding, purdah is basically an attitudinal matter rather than pre-scribed form of dress – an attitude that we find congenial. The next day I suggested to Mujeeb and Hamid that there seems to be considerable lat-itude with respect to purdah within the Ahmadi-Muslim community. This was greeted by an initial silence followed by the explanation that Alim had converted to Ahmadiyyat only two years before – he had been motivated to convert when he read *Conscience and Coercion* – and there-fore had much to learn about the intricacies of fully appropriate Ahmadi behaviour. The implied message was that they did not approve of the more liberal and relaxed approach to purdah adopted by Alim and Falak. Indeed I have never seen Mujeeb's wife nor Hamid's wife in spite of the surface appearance of liberality that they project.

Another example of the qualifying of purdah occurred when we shopped in Lahore for the bicycle we gave to the Tarik-i-Jadeed for the use of missionaries on furlough. After we finished making our purchase we were invited upstairs to the shopkeeper's home for tea and refresh-ments. His daughter-in-law, who joined us, appeared without the cus-tomary veil covering her face. Our hosts took note of our surprise and explained that given my mature years, the presence of my wife, and the respect in which we were held, we could be treated as family members to whom the conventional strictures of purdah did not apply. We were delighted. It is worth observing, however, that the shopowner's wife and mother did not come out to join us but remained in another room where they were visited by Peggy.

Sometime after our dinner with Alim and Falak, I raised the matter of gender with the murabhi, or missionary of the congregation, in Islam-abad. We agreed that there appears to be a fair amount of latitude within Ahmadiyyat respecting the dress that constitutes purdah, and we agreed further on an axiological absolute about the proper value and meaning that underlies the institution of purdah, namely, that feminine modesty and decorum correlate with masculine respect for womanhood. Beneath this there seems to be an often unspoken apprehension that without the restraining institution of purdah, the human sexual impulse would burst out unrestrained and wreak social havoc. But assuming this bedrock commitment to the value and essential meaning of purdah, there could then be different expressions of what degree of covering is required – a difference that would be culturally, and perhaps even subjectively, conditioned. This I took to be the murabhi's message.

In fact it turned out not to be what the missionary was suggesting. Certainly he agreed that the underlying and absolute value of purdah is the segregation of the sexes in such a way as to ensure feminine modesty, masculine control of male sexuality, and hence a secure and stable social life. But he was not saying that within this absolute existential value there was a variety of options respecting dress. That there is diversity is unquestionable but this he views as differences motivated by different levels of understanding and growth within the faith. There is a dress ideal and that is the full burqa, head covering, and veil that ideally leaves only the eyes exposed to the public world. Deviations from this ideal are precisely that – deviations that are not to be excoriated, persecuted, and prosecuted but simply acknowledged as human failings in understanding or commitment. What is important is the "direction" in which a person is moving. If one is moving towards ever fuller covering, it is still to be morally approved of even if one has not yet reached the ideal. On the other hand, if one is moving away from full covering then one is moving in a morally negative direction. Consequently, while this view does accommodate diversity of dress, it does so within the context of an absolute that pertains not only to attitudinal value but also ideally to overt expression or form of dress. This is what I call the Rabwah model, which is the conservative interpretation of what purdah entails. Clearly people like Alim and Falak have a different understanding.

Gender from the Perspective of a Professional Woman

One evening we had a visit from Dr Qureshi and later from Dr Nusrat Jahan. Dr Nusrat stayed until 10:00, which by Pakistani standards is late. She is an extraordinary woman, cheerful, buoyant, and fearless, who is also the person who regularly has to cut into the bellies of pregnant women for caesarean sections or hysterectomies or tubal ligations. She has retained close contact with the doctors who trained her in England and refers to them as consultants. We infer from this that she was highly regarded by them not only for her ebullient manner and her commitment but also for her high level of medical competency.

During the course of the evening Dr Nusrat reiterated some of the views she had shared with us at the hospital. As a Muslim woman, she holds that men and women have different natures. There is, of course, a universal spiritual nature but in addition to that there are peculiar qualities that characterize women and similarly distinctive qualities that characterize men. These gender particularities also imply vocational specialization. Men are by their divinely ordained nature better endowed to perform tasks in the public sphere that require a higher degree of strength and aggressiveness, and women by their nature are better equipped for nurturing roles involved in the maintenance of a home. But this gender-based vocational differentiation does not imply exclusivity. Women also are free to enter into the public sphere to pursue work in the "masculine" fashion, (just as men have domestic roles to perform as well. These were not carefully defined and further interviews may clarify what the different domestic roles for men are. It must be remembered that it is the men who prepare the meals for the thousands who attend the annual *jalsa*. The Ahmadi *jalsa* in Toronto in 2001 had more than nine thousand participants). According to Dr Nusrat, however, the priority remains for even the professional woman working outside the home to focus on her primary domestic role. With professional women this is made easier by the availability of servants to help with domestic chores. We have pointed out to our Pakistani friends that even well-paid bourgeois professionals in the West are forced to become their own menials – roofers, carpenters, plumbers, electricians, etc. Western women typically do all the household chores – washing, ironing, cooking, cleaning, etc. – that are, amongst the professional classes in Pakistan, relegated to servants. But Dr Nusrat was clear that women should not pursue a public career at the expense of their divinely ordained domestic obligation.

As we have seen, the corollary of this legitimation of the working woman is the permissibility of genders mixing at the workplace. What is not permitted is social mixing – that is to say, the mixing of the sexes in other than the formal framework of job obligations. I pointed out that this may be an artificial distinction: in the West certainly it is highly likely that most instances of adultery originate in the workplace and not in social settings such as a Saturday evening barbecue or a dinner party at which couples entertain one another. This Dr Nusrat recognized. The rationale for the strictures on dress in the work setting and the mixing of men and women is the danger of undisciplined sexuality. Her judgment is that men are by nature polygamous and that the advantage of Islam is that it acknowledges this and allows it with the proviso that men also assume responsibility for those with whom they have sex. Some Islamic commentators, however, seem to be more distressed about aggressive female sexuality than they are about man's polygamous nature. This Dr Nusrat also acknowledged as a force in human relationships and therefore as an additional reason for proceeding cautiously in relating the sexes one to the other, a caution that she believes is most fittingly expressed in the Islamic institution of purdah.

But this reduction of the risk of adultery and family fragmentation comes with a social cost. What's more, assaults on family integrity, responsibility, and nurturance are more distressing, arguably, than sexual peccadilloes, although we recognize that for many people the two are causally related. The Ahmadi scheme seems to assume that adultery has got to issue in marital breakup and family disintegration.

The lack of symmetry in our social relations in Rabwah was manifest in the way Peggy was allowed to accompany me to every one of our meetings, and on the one occasion that she did not, the director of the institution I was visiting expressed surprise and regret that she had not come. Peggy was permitted and encouraged to take part in all the exchanges and her views were welcomed. I pointed out the fundamental injustice of Muslim women being deprived of this opportunity. On the other hand, often when men and women are together in Western social settings, men dominate the conversation with the result that women are in effect excluded from the exchange. Still, it is hard for us to conceive of social relations in which one gender is by cultural definition deprived of active engagement because of apprehension about the marital, sexual, and social risks of permitting integration of the sexes.

Purdah as a Constraint on Adultery and Social Disarray

Although I was more interested in the personal testimony of so aged a patriarch of the Ahmadi movement, I asked Mirzah Abdul Haq, the ninety-five-year-old amir of Sargoda, for his views on purdah and the line of reasoning used to justify it. I realized, of course, that in an ultimate sense no justification is necessary; one must only submit to the will of God who has ordered the institution of the segregation of men and women. But the amir immediately said that there are good reasons for purdah and with surprising candour detailed his understanding, which was basically the Ahmadi Muslim perception of the role and power of the sexual instinct. He explained that of all instincts this is the most difficult to regulate. Men are drawn to female beauty with the corollary desire to reach out and sexually possess the desirable one. In the course of our discussion I acknowledged the social disarray that can be caused by unconstrained sexual license and the practice of adultery, which threatens to destroy family unity and cause discord within the community. He did not emphasize this particular social implication but rather the devotional importance of channelling all one's energies towards God. Without regulation of the sexual instinct one cannot reach God; the same love that men show towards women is the love that they should direct towards God. (This struck me as a peculiarly Hindu argument: some yogis claim that one uses the same energies for sex and for meditation, and to squander this finite pool of energy on sex deflects one from the single-minded meditation that leads to the realization of the unity of the true self with the universal spirit.) Since humans are born to have a personal relationship with God – to come under his protection and to be his obedient servant – then priority must be given to realizing this essential aim of human existence. This means, accordingly, that one must divert love of beauty and sexual passion from the woman and direct those emotions towards God. In order to save yourself, the amir said, it is necessary to put restraints on the eyes, the ears, and the heart, which is the most difficult of all.

This terror of sex amongst Ahmadi Muslims is a hard-headed, realistic assessment of the imperious claims of sexuality in human life. They do not need Freud to apprise them of the pervasiveness and urgency of sex and its instinctive thrust towards fulfillment if not repressed or sublimated. It is this recognition of the clamant nature of sexual desire that underlies the restrictions on free social mixing. From our discussion I gathered that the amir (in common with most if not all of the Ahmadi leaders with whom we have spoken) saw social mixing as an unnecessary provocation of the sexual appetites with all their destructive potencies, should they lead to premarital or adulterous sexual unions.

The amir added, however, that there is no intrinsic prohibition on a woman's participation in the public sphere provided that purdah could be strictly observed. He gave the example of his daughter-in-law, who prior to her marriage had worked for the Ministry of Foreign Affairs. She was designated for a post in France on condition that she abandon purdah. This she refused to do on principle and, as a consequence, resigned from the ministry. That had been in the early 1980s.

In line with the testimony of other Ahmadis informants, the amir stated that the pursuit of a public career for a women is subordinate in priority to the domestic roles of mother and wife, which constitute a woman's principal responsibility. The home is the source of happiness, and ideally a woman should restrict herself to the domestic sphere provided the husband has enough resources to allow her to do so. The amir believed that children always suffer if their mother works outside the home, and that that loss is far greater than the loss of additional money. Thus, it is desirable to avoid a public role when one is married unless economic stringency dictates otherwise. This appeals to the Islamic ideal, which is in tension with the counterclaim amongst some Ahmadis that working outside the home is allowable. It seems hard to avoid the conclusion that much of the leadership is working with a double level of Islamic obedience – an ideal that would typically require a woman to stay at home with children and husband, on the one hand, and an accommodation to a public vocation in situations of necessity (shading off into personal preference) on the other, but even here safeguarded by the proviso that purdah be observed.

In my view, the assertion that a relationship is purely platonic is usually an obfuscating expression of self-delusion: I largely agree with the epigram that there is no such thing as platonic relations. There are, of course, relations between the sexes that are devoid of any sexual interest or desire but they are rarely, if ever, relationships that one would characterize as possessing that degree of friendship that one would designate as platonic. Where there is a strong spiritual connection and the sharing intimacy and mutuality characteristic of friendships, there is typically an undercurrent of sexual attraction that acts as the physiological and psychological infrastructure for the creation of the relationship of friendship. It seems the course of wisdom and self-knowledge to admit that this is the case, which still leaves open the question what to do with the detection of underlying feelings of a sexual nature. Accordingly, I conceded to the amir the validity of the Ahmadi Muslim discernment of the enormous power of latent sexual feelings that can characterize seemingly innocent social mixing. The Ahmadis' recognition of this presence (speaking from the human point of view and not from the point of view of divine ordination) accounts for their imposition of austere restraints on the degree of contact that can exist between men and women. The deleterious cost of this, however, is the impoverishment (as we judge it) of human fellowship in that women are excluded from those areas of social intercourse that fall outside the strict definition of public professional duty.

I had asked the amir how, in the exercise of his pastoral role, he viewed the discovery of adultery, and whether the exposure of adultery elicited a pastoral strategy of encouraging forgiveness and reconciliation. His reply was clear and brief: adultery seldom came to light and should be hidden. This I thought was a very realistic assessment of the incapacity of human nature to accept the psychic threat of a mate's sexual experience with another person. His attitude was that if one lamentably lapses into sin, one should at least have the good sense and decency to hide it from the world and not parade it in some self-indulgent orgy of "openness." This was not a denial of the occurrence of adultery but only of the unwisdom of allowing it to come to light. We have no way of knowing the extent of adulterous relations amongst Muslims in general and the Ahmadis specifically. In one interview I remarked that it seemed extraordinarily difficult if not impossible to initiate extramarital sexual contact, to which the answer was, it happens. I chose not to pursue the matter, though we are certainly curious as to how it could possibly come about, given the restrictions on women's movements in either the domestic sphere, which includes shopping, or in some cases the professional sphere, generally limited to teaching and medical practice.

Implicit in the amir's point of view was the assumption that human nature is such that it cannot handle the psychic devastation of the discovery of a mate's infidelity and that the attendant pain and confusion, not to mention the assault on one's pride and social standing, are generally intolerable psychic and social burdens for people to bear.

I reflected later on my discussion with Mirzah Abdul Haq as I strolled in the rose court, enjoying the early morning light that is characteristic of the subcontinent and the refreshing air that still retained a bit of the evening chill but was already assuming a luxurious feeling that portends growing warmth as the sun rises. Things seem to come to life slowly especially in this post-Ramadan period. The streets were not yet filled with traffic and consequently the dust levels were low and the air more transparent and bracing. The customary birdsong, dominated by the insistent cawing of the crows, could be heard in the tall willow trees that surround the compound and in the neem trees within the compound. This for me is probably the most beautiful and satisfying time of the day, perhaps even more so than the late afternoon and early evenings when the sun is slanting low through the fields and through the trees and turns the poppy petals into iridescent jewels as the light filters through their porous structure.

It is necessary to probe further to uncover the motivations that underlie the Ahmadi insistence on a strict level of purdah not only with respect to segregation of the sexes and the prohibition on social mixing but also with respect to the extreme form of covering and veiling that is the Ahmadi standard.

There is on the one hand what I might call, somewhat melodramatically, the terror of sex. The assumption, as already noted, is that human beings and men in particular are by nature sexually aggressive and even rapacious in their physical desires; were it not for divinely ordained constraints that severely limit the amount of contact between the sexes, there would be a high degree of sexual exploitation and even attacks upon women. There is also, when pressed, an acknowledgment that female sexuality can also be a clamant force, but the emphasis falls on women's weakness and vulnerability when placed against male strength and sexual aggressiveness. Ayoub, the Ahmadi businessman who drove Peggy and me over the salt mountains from Rabwah to Islamabad, spoke of the need to protect one's wife from the "greedy eyes of men." The fact that I derive satisfaction from the complimentary male attention paid to my wife would probably not be well understood or sympathized with.

The Muslims' sexual apprehension is not simply about the prospect of unbridled male sexuality. There is also acknowledgment of the deleterious social consequences of the sexual contact that, in their judgement, would inevitably result from free social mixing. Again, the assumption is that the sexual attraction that would result from such social contact between the sexes would lead to adultery – a most grievous sin for which fundamentalist Islam has sought to reassign the penalty of death by stoning. This punishment would not be countenanced by the Ahmadis but it discloses the gravity with which Muslims view the violation of marriage through adulterous relations. Because of the ideological commitment of Muslims to the stable social order that results from following shari'a – the straight highway that God had ordained for human behaviour – the possibility of social anarchy and disruption that adultery raises begets extreme apprehension. In support of this concern, Muslims point to the disintegration of social relations in the West where the high incidence of premarital sex has led to broken families, single-parent families, disease, mental breakdown, and all sorts of associated social ills. The case they make is certainly intelligible and could be analyzed in terms of a cost/benefit equation. The high social cost of family breakdown, which they view as inevitably consequent upon adultery, requires that the corresponding price of social inhibitions and restraints be paid in order to obtain the benefit of social peace and harmonious marriage relations.

A different cost/benefit analysis could be done, however, in which the liabilities of extreme segregation of the sexes could be construed as too high a price to be paid for the avoidance of adultery and its consequences of psychic distress and social disruption. There is no question that in either analysis there is a cost to be paid, and the resolution of these competitive views can only be reached by relying on the authority of one value judgment over the other. In the Islamic case it is not a matter of subjective choices but rather fidelity to the revealed word of God. But even that may be too simple since we have already noted that there is considerable degree of latitude among Muslims in divining or stipulating precisely what the principle of purdah entails. Ayoub has intimated that probably only five percent of women in Islamabad still wear the veil, though whether they would see this as an abandonment of purdah is problematic: there is debate as to how purdah is properly expressed in the modern world.

That adultery need not be a calamitous event with irredeemably negative consequences does not seem to enter the Muslim equation. Whether additional unspoken motives are at work here, such as culturally bequeathed patriarchal values that unconsciously define women as male property over which men have custodial rights, need not arrest us now. My intention as always is to grasp the self-understanding of Ahmadis, and so I have restricted myself to a description of their stated legitimation of purdah under the rubrics of the terror of sex and the social and familial devastation attendant upon adultery.

Any notion of tantric transcendence that moves beyond rigid dichotomous thinking about good and bad, faith and unfaith, chaste and unchaste, is absent from the explicit rationale of the Ahmadi leadership. Their thinking seems oriented along a characteristic Semitic line of moral dualism between the will of God and the disobedience of humanity, the divine and the satanic, good and bad, understood not only as the opposition of virtues, values, and dispositions but also as explicit external forms of behaviour. In this world view of moral dualism expressed in explicit legal prohibitions and prescriptions, there is little room for the accommodations that situational ethical thinking provides.

Islam's moral demands aim not only at external performance and conformity to a revealed pattern of behaviour but also at the inculcation of moral virtue and attitudes. Accordingly, the first demand with respect to purdah is the internalization of the disposition to act always with decorum, modesty, and chastity. However, Islam does not stop at the level of intentions and moral attitudes. It also moves on to particular forms of behaviour that are deemed to be commensurate with required moral attitudes. This is where the problem emerges. For many Muslims, Islam is looked upon as stipulating specific forms of dress and covering that are deemed to be the morally correct manifestation of the internal attitude of proper decorum between the sexes. Over against this view, others contend that there is latitude in deciding what form of covering is, for a given person, in that culture, an appropriate manifestation of modesty. Our friend Rafiq holds that the particular form of dress is culturally determined and shaped by historical epochs. He points out (what has so frequently been drawn to my attention) that Muslim women sitting before Hazoor on the floor in his question-and-answer periods in London had their faces completely uncovered, and that this is Islamic. The other example that is frequently adduced is that of women in rural areas who cannot be encumbered by the long burqa and head scarf and veil that typify women in the town of Rabwah. The rural women's work requires that they be less well covered in order to perform their tasks with the men in the fields and they would typically wear just a long gown or sari.

It appeared at first glance that we were dealing with a fairly common-place distinction in ethics — that the only uncompromisable absolute is the kernel of core attitude or virtues (in this case modesty and respect), while the husk of external behaviour can adopt varying forms depending on historical and cultural circumstances. But this too turned out to be simplistic as we encountered what have been called middle axioms. Though the demand for modesty and discipline is unconditional, there are other norms approaching an absolute, in the form of an ideal mode of dress, that, all things being equal, ought to be emulated. According to the Qur'an, not only should the breasts be covered so as to hide their swelling which would be an enticement to the covetous eyes of men (Sura 24:31–2) but the face or portions thereof should also be covered. What can be excluded from covering according to the Qur'an are the eyes and the nose. There is more debate about the mouth, the conclusion apparently being that where it is necessary to uncover the mouth for the easy passage of breath, then the mouth need not be covered. When I asked what remained to be covered, I was told the forehead and the cheeks, the lower chin, and perhaps even the mouth, all of which should be covered, if not with the veil, at least with a scarf drawn across the lower face.

Consequently, it is ambiguous to say that all alternative forms of garb, from the austere, full black burqa, abri, and veil of the Rabwah women to the unveiled women of Bosnia, to the loose-fitting gowns of the un-veiled peasants of rural Punjab are all equally Islamic, in spite of Rafiq's insistence that they are. Under persistent questioning it emerges that they do not represent an equal approximation to the Qur'anic Islamic ideal. Perhaps the solution is to say that they are all equally Islamic in that they share an underlying desire to observe a spiritual and moral decorum and restraint in relations between the sexes. Further, they may, in some compromisory ambivalent way, all be Islamic in the sense that they represent different accommodations to prevailing historical and cultural circumstances. They are not all equally Islamic, however, with respect to an Islamic ideal that enjoins not only the internalization of an appropriate attitude but also the assumption of a particular form of dress that entails covering most of the face and body.

During a long interview with Maulana Sultan Mahmood Anwar, the nazir of the Islaho Irshad Markaziyya (Director of Preaching and Religious Education inside Pakistan; the word for preaching would normally be *tabligh* but the Ahmadis are not allowed to use this word because it would contradict the legislation against proselytizing), we discussed the notion that there are two constraints on women's movements and activities in Islam. The first is the proper performance of her homemaking role and the second is that the principle of purdah not be violated. Respecting the first, we agreed on what I take to be a standard Islamic perspective on women's natures and roles, namely, that women have a specific nature resulting from God's creative wisdom that uniquely qualifies them to fulfill the domestic role. Maulana Sultan characterized this as the internal maintenance of the home. The distinctive male nature, by contrast, equips man for an external role in the public sphere, which entails providing and safeguarding the family income and undertaking other matters that involve the political and economic life outside the home. The basic principle that the women's primary domestic role is child-bearing, child-rearing, and homemaking does not in itself preclude activity outside the home, whether it be construed as paid employment or as the voluntary activity for the community that characterizes the lives of most Ahmadi women. Such volunteer work typically involves the Lejna with its various departments such as children's education, social services, and pregnancy counselling. But all of these activities outside the home, whether paid professional work or volunteer service, have to be, as Maulana Sultan said, in pursuit of "worthy aims and worthy purposes." In other words, as long as it is compatible with the divinely ordained primary domestic aim, then women are by no means bound twenty-four hours a day to the house as some stereotypes of Islamic women would have it.

This led to the second principle that regulates women's activity – the mandate for segregation, or purdah. My question was this: if a woman's pursuit of a worthy purpose outside the home, consistent with the primary value of child rearing and homemaking, should entail the abandonment of purdah as practised strictly in Rabwah, would it constitute a prohibition on that purpose? I proposed a hypothetical case in which a woman needed, for the economic well-being of her children, to work outside the home in a context that would necessitate mixing with males beyond the excluded categories, that is to say, beyond those males that she would not be allowed to marry, and that further required the relinquishment of purdah – burqa, hijab, and veil. What would Islam permit this woman to do? There was some hesitation here, but under repeated formulations of the question the answer emerged that even purdah is compromisable. This implies that the primary principle guiding women's activity is not purdah in the sense of segregation and the stipulation of an invariable form of dress.

Given that purdah is so important to Ahmadi Muslim practice, it was inevitable that some way out of the dilemma of compromisable purdah would be found. It took the form of saying that although purdah might be sacrificed in the short run, the whole society would eventually come to see the wisdom of the strict boundaries between the genders that Islam draws and move towards the introduction of purdah. I pointed out that in Canada what we see is the reverse: not Ahmadi Islam changing the larger society but the dominant culture bringing about an alteration in the definition of purdah and what it entails in a practical sense. A growing number of Ahmadi women were working outside the home in contexts where headscarves, let alone the burqa, were impracticable or simply no longer acceptable to the Ahmadi women themselves.

The Ahmadis, however, generally seem reluctant to impose exclusive standards of behaviour, frequently citing the Qur'anic text that there is no compulsion in religion. Nevertheless, it does seem that the underlying view favours a highly traditionalist relegation of women to the domestic sphere and separation from contact with men outside the excluded categories. Women, of course, are accorded large roles in society; their views are sought and expressed in various congregational meetings. But they are expressed, as we have seen, either over a public-address system or from behind a curtain. The Ahmadi leadership remains adamant about the dangers of and prohibition on free social mixing.

Peggy pointed out with great courtesy but with strong conviction how awkward it is to be allowed to sit with me in the company of three other men and take part in an intellectual exchange, whereas their wives are not. One man responded that his wife would not be interested in that kind of discussion. Then, under Peggy's prodding, he said that if it were a case where his wife could be helpful in such a discussion, she certainly could be present. But the de facto practice in a place like Rabwah is strongly segregationist. For example, when we went to Dr Nusrat Jahan's for dinner, I never saw her mother, who, being older and very conservative, avoided greeting me. Peggy, however, went in and had a long conversation with her. When we left she sent her greetings and good wishes, but still I did not see her at any point. I never see any of the wives of the men with whom we move about so engagingly.

Peggy and I are of the conviction that this is not a way of life that will eventually be appreciated and emulated in the West but rather a way of life that would be impossible to maintain in the secularized context of the West. At the time of this research, Pakistani women in the major cities like Lahore and Islamabad were relinquishing the veil and apparently this tendency will increase as more Muslim women move towards Euroamerican culture with its doctrine of freedom between the genders. One day we were talking to a teacher who was quite casual about letting her *dupatta* drop away from her face, both outside when we were organizing the children for a group photograph and then as we stood in the doorway of the school office. We also noted that when we arrived at Dr Nusrat's home, she let her veil drop. This was the first time in all the hours we had spent together that I saw the lower part of her face. But we surmise that when she went in to greet her mother in her room she was admonished, for when she came out she had covered her face with the veil and remained veiled throughout the evening even while sitting at dinner, where both she and her sixteen-year-old daughter had to eat by discreetly lifting their veils from time to time to put food into their mouths.

Once again, I could not restrain an inward dismay at what Peggy and I feel is a socially impoverishing separation of the genders that precludes the mutual enrichment that occurs when women and men can talk together freely. At the same time I remained aware of a point I made elsewhere, that segregation allows women to grow and flourish in male dominated spaces. The right to separate "women only" space that many Western feminists have fought hard for has always been available to

Muslim women. While I have tended to emphasize the fact that Ahmadi women are shut out from men's space, I recognized that they might see it the other way around – that men are shut out from women's space, which has its own intricacies and power relations.

The Lejna, or women's association headquarters, is a building with numerous offices and an enormous gymnasium and meeting hall. In one room four or five young women were sorting out bales of cloth to be given to poor families to sew into new clothing for the festival of Eid-al-Fitr. We gathered in the office of the vice-president of the association. She happened to be Mirza Ghulam Ahmad's wife, as I mentioned earlier, and a woman with very attractive eyes, which was all one could see since she wore her veil over her nose almost to the bottom of the eyes. Peggy had met her before and discovered that she is a poet. We were served tea, which we had learned to accept even though it was Ramadan and the Ahmadis themselves were fasting. Ghulam Ahmad, who is a fluent English speaker, responded to most of our questions although he checked with his wife, who clearly understood English as well, in Urdu before responding to our questions. He pointed out that Islam does not expect women to be closed up within the confines of their homes and that most Ahmadi women devote a great deal of time to the volunteer work of the Lejna. Ghulam Ahmad's wife is probably on the extreme end of the spectrum of volunteer commitment, but even when her children were smaller she devoted a great deal of time to the work of the organization and, once they were grown, spent as much time in volunteer work as she would have spent in a paying full-time job. The Ahmadis point to involvement in the women's organization, which appears to be a powerful, efficiently administered body, to meet the criticism that Islam sequesters women within the four walls of their home. On the question of purdah, understood as the requirement to wear concealing clothing, Ghulam Ahmad said that his wife's dress represented the ideal, with the face and forehead fully covered and the eyes alone being allowed to show, though not all Ahmadi Muslim women had to follow the same pattern, and exceptions were certainly allowed for those living in foreign cultures.

One evening I took a solitary walk from the western outskirts of Rabwah to where the habitations give way to an expanse of green fields that stretch away into infinity. The lowering sun cast silhouettes of various trees including the drooping arms of palms. In the very far distance the conical peak of one of the rock formations in the direction of Sargoda gave the impression of a transplanted Mount Fuji. On my left, stretching off into the distance through the fields, was a railway embankment. As I stood there enjoying the tranquility of the evening, I thought of the Indian film *Patar Panjali*, in which a village boy goes one day on a long trek across the fields to an area he has never been to before and, breaking through the cane, discovers the railway embankment and witnesses for the first time the thundering belching presence of a locomotive. I turned right along a hard-packed dirt track and came to a little hamlet consisting of the characteristic adobe dwelling with compounds in front occupied by numerous water buffalo, goats, and even camels, and with ducks swimming about in a stagnant, murky pool. I finally arrived at the highway and retraced my steps back to Rabwah. Nearing home, I cut through some lanes past the principal's house and encountered Anas Ahmad, who inquired after Peggy's and my health and asked whether we had had a happy Eid. I replied that we had gone to the Eid prayer at 8:30 in the morning at the al-Aqsa mosque and he said that he had seen us there. I reported that we had gone to Naseer's for dinner. In many ways it had been a very quiet day for us in the midst of a cultural setting wherein Eid seemed to be the chief celebratory social event. We had been deeply moved by the arrival early in the morning of an enormous fancy cake, half of which we took over to Naseer's home along with a collection of sweets and dates that we had bought down in the bazaar and a bowl of special pudding, made only for Eid, that had been sent over by Monsoor Khan's wife. After we returned from Naseer's home in the afternoon we felt a little bereft and wondered what all our other friends of the community were doing for their Eid celebration.

This episode precipitated a discussion between Peggy and myself about the dynamics that might be at work in this cultural situation. Peggy pointed out that everyone we had spoken to or interviewed had seen her face, whereas I had never looked upon the faces of their wives. This prompted us to reflect about the power of purdah even in situations where relationships, as far as we could tell, had become cordial, respectful, and even affectionate. Peggy wondered why our Ahmadi friends and interlocutors could not simply declare us family on the occasions when we saw each other, given our mature age and the fact that many of the restraints had been eliminated already by the way we had moved around the community. But this evinces the power of legal morality within a community that is committed to the principle of purdah in a cultural setting that gives it the fairly specific form of burqa, headscarf, and veil. The typical feature of legal morality is that is does not readily lend itself to flexibility. There is, of course, a degree of flexibility amongst the Ahmadis, but it results from a process of casuistry rather than from an existential situational decision. I define casuistry as a use of rules to define rules. A clear example that most Christians would be familiar with is the Jewish law "Thou shalt not do any work on the Sabbath." The question immediately emerges as to what constitutes work, and here the rabbinic casuistic process is invoked to specify which activity is work and therefore a violation of the Sabbath and which activity is not. The outcome is, for example, a definition of a Sabbath journey. One answer to the question "How much walking constitutes work?" is that any travelling beyond the amount of walking required to get one to the neighbourhood synagogue for prayer constitutes forbidden work. Similarly, how much rope tying constitutes work? One casuistic answer is that any knot that can be undone with one hand does not constitute work.

Turning back to the Ahmadi case, what we observe is a rather restricted form of flexibility that employs the casuistic process to interpret the application of a specific general law. Assuming for the moment that there had been a genuine desire to host Peggy and me at some of the larger Eid gatherings, the members were prevented by the absence of a rule that would have permitted greater liberality with respect to the permission of outside men to look upon the faces of their wives or daughters. Because so many of the people with whom we had been associated were leaders within the Ahmadi community, it would be incumbent upon them to maintain the standards of the *jama'at* and not be seen confusing the pious by displaying a mode of behaviour that might be construed as a violation of purdah. It may be that what was at work was the inhibition of an impulse of hospitality and openness towards us by the requirements of a legal morality that had no rules to permit the suspension of purdah in our case.

It should also be noted that in our meal with Naseer, purdah was largely observed as Naseer, his son, and I took our food alone in one room while Peggy and his wife and two daughters took their food in another room. It is clear that the price paid by the family in this case was the inability to eat their Eid meal together. But such are the trade-offs required by fidelity to purdah. Whereas Naseer might have been prepared, perhaps out of consideration for us given the lateness of the invitation, to sacrifice family unity on that occasion, others might not have been prepared to do so on what was for them the most important family gathering of the year.

Precedents in Hadith

I had asked Anas Ahmad for Islamic legitimations of male participation in the domestic sphere and female participation in the public sphere and these were now provided. In one Hadith the witness was asked how the Prophet used his time and he replied that the Prophet divided his day into three parts. The first was for *ibadat*, or service of God, the second for his family, and the third for himself. This latter category was subdivided into two parts. The first was time devoted purely to the self and the second time devoted to works of charity towards others. From the statement that the Prophet gave one-third of his time to his family, the lesson is extrapolated that Muhammad participated in domestic chores, and since his behaviour is Sunna (customary precedent), it provides the paradigm for ideal Muslim male behaviour. Just as Muhammad was neither excluded from nor forbidden to participate in the domestic sphere of the home, neither are present day Muslim men.

In another Hadith, Aishah, the Prophet's third and favourite wife, relates how Muhammad would help in the home. Another Hadith relates how the Prophet would mend his own clothes and shoes. The upshot of all this is that the Prophet's exemplary behaviour is the warrant for male participation in the domestic sphere. Then there is the Hadith telling how Aishah worked in the public sphere when she and her female companions went out after the battle to collect and treat the wounded and, further, how she and the women defended the camp against enemy soldiers. These Hadiths provide a model for feminine participation in the public sphere. On the historical plane, Aishah led a revolt against Ali, the Prophet's son-in-law, when he became the fourth caliph, but this was not brought to our attention by any Ahmadi.

What we have through these Hadiths, then, are two moral paradigms that legitimate participation by both genders in both realms of human activity. This does not preclude specialization or concentration of one gender in one area and the other in another sphere. While Islam does not exclude either gender from working in both areas of life, it does emphasize that the main responsibility of the female lies in the domestic sphere while the main obligation of the male is in the public sphere.

Purdah in the Khalifa's Judgment

I may have been investing my time fruitlessly in numerous interviews investigating the nature and requirement of purdah inasmuch as in a hierarchical system like Ahmadiyyat the final and definitive word must come from the khalifa. In his statement before the annual convention of the Lejna on 27 December 1982 the fourth khalifa expounded the proper understanding of Islamic purdah (see Appendix 2). It is necessary to point out, however, that certain ambiguities remain that may be ascribed to the diverse expositions of various Ahmadi authors and spokespersons within the community.

The Qur'anic warrant for purdah is Sura Nur *vss* 31–2 in Sura 24. The khalifa pointed out that there is a diversity of purdah with respect to the external covering of the garments. There is the burqa, which is the long overcoat that is then surmounted by a kind of kerchief that goes down the back and the sides of the face, and a veil that is normally worn across the nose, leaving only the eyes exposed. Alternatively, there is the Afghan shuttlecock burqa that falls from the crown of the head to the ground. There is also the chador, the large enveloping shawl or drape that in the fourth khalifa's judgment was still acceptable, though less desirable because of the difficulty of wearing it in such a way as to provide authentic Islamic purdah. The chador was acceptable if it was draped over the head and drawn down over the face so that both cheeks were covered. It also goes without saying that the cleavage of the breast must also be covered, and this is typically accomplished by drawing the chador beneath the chin. The khalifa's objection to this was that it encouraged a custom of allowing the chador to fall to the shoulders, exposing both the hair and the face, thus becoming not a garment of modest covering and protection but rather another sartorial element of decoration and embellishment. The burqa makes it much easier to maintain proper Islamic purdah, although the chador is acceptable – particularly in Western societies where women are heavily engaged in economic life and find the burqa and its associated head covering less practical. However, the chador type of covering, which we found typical of Iran, is already in vogue in Pakistani villages as the women go to the fields carrying food for their husbands or water from the wells.

I referred above to the ambiguity of this speech. There are various ways of interpreting its ambiguity. First, we may be confronted with a two-level moral standard analogous to the medieval Christian distinction between *praecepta evangelica* (the moral precepts of the gospel) and *consilia evangelica*, where the *consilia evangelica*, or counsels of perfection, are seen as works of supererogation that go above and beyond the moral demands or precepts that are laid upon every Christian. Applying this to the Ahmadi case, we might conclude that the chador could be viewed as a precept that is acceptable as a minimal standard of Islamic covering for women while the burqa would be a counsel of perfection, that is to say, a work of supererogation that represents a higher level of discipline and commitment. There were hints of this interpretation when the khalifa pointed out that the women in the family of the Promised Messiah in Qadian always wore the burqa and deemed it necessary to protect their sanctity from the degrading gaze of lustful men.

A second interpretation is that we have a diversity that is culturally relative. In a strict Pakistani cultural milieu where Islamic standards are prevalent, the fuller covering provided by the burqa and veil is more applicable and therefore to be preferred. In Western societies, given the manner in which women are already uncovered almost to the point of nakedness in some cases, and given the greater involvement of women in the workforce, an appropriate Islamic purdah could be the simpler chador, even though it leaves most of the face exposed. On this interpretation there is no question of a higher or lower standard but simply the appropriation of a standard or norm that is relative and appropriate to the particular culture in which one lives.

Yet another possible interpretation is that beyond a certain undefined and minimal standard of covering, the essential dimension of purdah is an internal attitude of modesty, decorum, and dignity, thus leaving to individual conscience the question of what degree of covering, in the particular circumstances in which one finds oneself, is the proper outer expression of the inner and spiritual grace of modesty and chastity. It must be borne in mind that the khalifa's speech was in 1982 and it is quite possible that his immersion in the life of the West since his flight from Pakistan to London in 1984, caused his views to shift in the direction of greater liberality. This is certainly the way the matter was presented to us by the young couple in Islamabad who believed that the khalifa would uphold their own more liberal understanding of purdah. A problematical dimension of our research conclusions derives perhaps from extrapolating excessively from Rabwah, which, being a sort of Vatican of the Ahmadi movement, allows and expects the public expression of the Ahmadi understanding of authentic and ideal Islamic life in a way not possible elsewhere. It seems, moreover, that a conservative ethos and interpretation predominates in Rabwah. Whether the situation may emerge in which a conservative faction finds itself in opposition to a liberal-leaning khalifa inspired by the exigencies of Islamic missionary work on a grand scale in the West remains an open question.

part three
POLITICS

LEFT: Dar al Zikr in Lahore, the principal Ahmadi mosque in Pakistan

RIGHT: Nino with our friends Mujeeb-Ur-Rahman, a lawyer from Rawalpindi, and Amir Hamid Nasrullah Khan from Lahore

LEFT: Nino with the amir of Sargodha,
who was ninety-three years old in 1995
and still vigorous and intellectually alert

RIGHT: Author with Anas Ahmad
exchanging views in the courtyard
of our guesthouse

LEFT: The duties of the men who guard the Rabwah Treasury include banging the brass gong each hour on the hour twenty-four hours a day

RIGHT: We were deeply touched by the gathering of all the Tehrik-i-jadeed staff to bid us goodbye upon our departure from Rabwah

CHAPTER FIVE

Islam, Politics, and the Ahmadis

After tea with the editor of the *Al Fazl Daily*, during which we were served the customary cups of sweet *dudh chai*, or milk tea, and pound cake and cookies from the local bakery, we visited a large exhibition of Ahmadi history and life that was prepared as a 1989 centenary project. Unfortunately there was a power cut, so that we were left midway through in near darkness. The visit had to be brought to an end, but we had got a sense of how the Ahmadis view their history. They had collected hundreds of photographs of early members of the movement, including not only the customary portraits of the Founder and the khalifas but also of the early companions – those who first made their *bai'at*, or pledge of loyalty, to the khalifa and acknowledged his status as the Promised Messiah and Mahdi, who had come to reform Islam and to inaugurate the new period of prophecy.

Islamic Political Theory

Malcolm Kerr in his *Islamic Reform: The Political and Legal Theories of Muhammad Abduh and Rashid Rida*, uses severe language to criticize Muslim political and legal theory. He condemns the classical viewpoint of the caliphate and jurisprudence as "inadequate" and "deficient" because of their inability to move in an agreed-upon manner from the ideal revelational sources of personal and social law to their application in the concrete positive law of the community. Classical theorists seem to have been unable to break out of the cocoon of an ideal vision of divine sovereignty over the totality of human life disclosed pre-eminently in the Qur'an and the Sunna of the Prophet, to the embodiment of shari'a in the practical, especially political, life of the community. Consequently, despite Muslim apologists' frequent appeal to their dissolution of the artificial Christian distinction between sacred and temporal spheres, Islamic history, in reality, presents us with a divine revelation that regulates mainly *ibadat* (ritual duties towards God) and acts of social status, especially those pertaining to the regulation of family life. The other, wider spheres of human life such as economics and politics are, in spite of all theological rhetoric to the contrary, abandoned to the autonomous power of rational calculation or the pursuit of special personal and collective interests.

Upon closer scrutiny, the frequent appeals to the Islamization of society turn out, I would suggest, to be rhetorical or metaphorical appeals. The Islamic boast that the religion of Muhammad advocates and reveals a way of life that encompasses the totality of human occupations and concerns may be true with respect to underlying motivations and values. A devout Muslim's aspiration should be to show forth a way of life that reflects the sovereignty of God over all spheres of human activity. When we try, however, to translate this affirmation of divine sovereignty over the totality of human existence into a concrete program of legislation, we encounter enormous difficulties. As long as our purview is restricted to ritual obligation or to matters of family law, the prohibitions and prescriptions are tolerably clear. However, the claim that shari'a extends to the economic and political spheres becomes a vacuous claim apart from the insistence that society should ideally be an integral society in the sense that it is in all respects organized around the principle of divine sovereignty and divine guidance. The specific application of this motivation of obedience to God is not clear, not only because there are divergent and competing legal schools with different viewpoints about what obedience entails in specific situations but also because it is by no means evident on the basis of Qur'an or Sunna what a particular divine mandate in a modern pluralistic society ought to be.

But the problem is not one that emerges only in the modern period. Almost from the beginning, Islam had to tailor its ideal vision of a society whose life is in every respect subject to the revealed will of God to the empirical necessities of state conflict and power. One solution has been to idealize and absolutize the period of the first four caliphs as the only Islamic period in which the unity of religion and state was embodied within history, but which remains only as an ideal to aspire to in the present and a kind of eschatological summons for the future. In the day-to-day responsibilities and conflicts of the state, however, decisions are made not on the basis of obedience to some revealed norm but on the calculation of the possibilities within the constraints and compromises of secular power.

The characterization of Islamic society as a theocracy, accordingly, is true only so far as it refers to an underlying set of religious motivations and aspirations. But between this theocratic ideal and the practical duties and obligations of the state there remains an enormous gulf. Theocracy becomes on a practical level largely irrelevant in the absence of any mediating mechanisms to interpret the meaning of God's rule in actual circumstances. A theocracy, or more properly a nomocracy, without such an interpretive or mediating agency or structure has little regulative force within a society other than as an ideal vision to motivate actions. In the absence, however, of concrete divine guidance, all societies function in much the same way – by working out untidy accommodations to conflicting sources of power within a society.

In spite of the accusations of the enemies of Ahmadiyyat that it is a political movement, the published testimony of Mirza Tahir Ahmad, Khalifatul Masih IV, is that Ahmadis do not need to control the levers of government but require only that whatever government there is govern according to principles of justice and maintain peace and order in the society. This seems to imply that Ahmadi political theory is prepared to sacrifice what is viewed as the essential unity of the political and the religious that lies at the heart of Islam and that is thought to have existed in the period of Muhammad and the Rightly Guided Companions. Muslims in this period of pristine and normative purity lived an ideal life, it is widely held, in which there was no separation between the demands of God in the ritual or religious field and in the political field. This integralist paradigm has everafter represented the ideal for Islamic society. Contemporary attempts at the creation or recreation of Islamic society are an attempt to repristinate that vision. The question then emerges how the Ahmadis justify the apparent abandonment of that normative vision in order to endorse a view of their own khalifa as one who rules over the spiritual and ritual matters of personal status such as marriage and divorce, or narrowly religious affairs of the community while relegating political sovereignty to non-Muslims.

Sacred Structures and Secularization

We may approach the question by asking whether vocational diversity within an Ahmadiyyat polity necessarily implies a division into autonomous spheres of sacred and secular. The experimental hypothesis that I proposed to our Ahmadi friends was that just as Islam recognizes a diversity of vocations between men and women, with women normatively exercising the child-caring duties within the domestic area and men exercising the duties of ruling and defending within the public one, even so the division between the narrowly religious role of the khalifa and the worldly rule of the prince or sovereign legitimates a diversity of callings – one spiritual and sacred, the other temporal and secular.

This analogy, however, needs to be unpacked more thoroughly to determine whether diversity of function or calling entails a two-sphere political theory of Islam involving two non-intersecting circles of activity. Even with respect to men and women the spheres are blurred, as in the Hadith relating how Aishah led the women in fighting against those who had infiltrated their camp, or when men share the domestic obligations. But, more importantly, it must be recognized that the vocational differentiation between men and women is integrated by their shared ordination by God. Accordingly, the boundaries between spiritual and secular are blurred by their shared obedience to the will of God.

Let me supply another metaphor. The body has a foot for walking and a hand for grasping; that is to say, these two members of the body have specialized functions. It is the same body, however, all of it, for the purpose of this analogy, controlled by the head. Similarly, there is one universe and one Supreme Head, God the Creator, Legislator, and Judge. This does not preclude the Ahmadi khalifa's dealing more or less exclusively with spiritual duties and the prince dealing with the duties of political power, but both are under the law of God. In Islam, there can be no autonomous sphere of worldly action. The danger from a religious point of view of the two-sphere type of political thinking is that the duties owed to God may come to be restricted to religious duties in the narrow sense that focus on the experience of prayer and pilgrimage, bearing witness, and teaching and preaching. The duties of the citizen in the state thus become divorced from an ultimate allegiance to God. On this view, functional differentiation of calling becomes, in effect, a truncation of God's sovereign rule over the entire universe.

It seems to me that Khalifa Mirza Tahir Ahmad, with his confidence in a universal law of natural justice, has minimized the value conflicts that exist in contemporary society – conflicts that allow social concord to exist only within the framework of a secular state. While the more or less neutral secular state may be agreeable to some religions, it can be accepted by integralist religious outlooks like Islam's only with great reservations. It may be, however, that the Ahmadi perspective, which at many points comes close to most Western social theory reflecting secularization as a way of dealing with the conflicts of religious diversity, is a cogent interpretation of Islam's worldly responsibilities. Within the Ahmadi system, this is entirely possible given that the process of prophetic revelation has not been closed and remains open for novel divine disclosures and guidance to the community through the khalifa.

Let me illustrate the conflicts and resolutions at work in this controversy with some current instances. Abortion legislation illustrates the difficulties posed by conflicting value systems and social programs in pluralistic, increasingly secular, societies. A prominent view among Christian opponents of abortion who look upon it as an act of murder of the innocent and therefore as unconditionally wrong is that the prohibition against abortion is not simply a matter of internal church discipline incumbent on those Christians who have appropriated this particular interpretation. Rather, they see it as a divine mandate that applies to the whole of humanity. Their pro-life stance is not regarded as one value possibility amongst a range of others, with each community of commitment living in terms of its own perceptions and values. Instead the structure of the cosmos dictates one and only one proper way of acting if one is to act in conformity with the natural order of things as this has come from the mind of God. This absolutist point of view does not allow a live-and-let-live attitude. The prohibition against abortion is not a matter of what is good for me but what is good for the world, for humankind. This is not regarded as a negotiable value dependent on the appropriation of alternative symbol systems; it is viewed as a way of life that is compatible with the intrinsic structure of reality and therefore mandatory for all citizens. We have, accordingly, the phenomenon of fundamentalist Christians in the United States abandoning their previous voluntary alienation from the political process on the basis of texts like "Come ye out and be separate" and instead adopting an activist role that seeks the transformation not just of the covenant community but of the entire society in the direction of their understanding of the divine will for the whole of creation.

Another example that lays bare the profound value conflicts that characterize a religiously pluralistic society in the womb of a predominantly secular state is the question of spousal benefits for homosexual couples. While this is rejected on religious grounds by a number of ecclesiastical bodies it is justified by advocates of the secular state as a necessary corollary of universal justice. There seems to be no way out of this dilemma that would satisfy everyone. I have argued elsewhere that the secular state is necessary in order to ensure social peace amongst religions that might otherwise, on the historical record, be at each other's throats. On the other hand, the advent of the secular state as a necessary neutral structure for religious and cultural diversity means that many of the convictions of religious persons will have to be sacrificed or held in abeyance.

This sacrifice will include not only specific religious symbolic events, such as the celebration of holy days like Christmas and Easter within state schools, but also certain aspects of social policy on abortion and homosexuality because they contradict the secular state's universalizing principles of justice.

In Islam's view of the state, secular government cannot be collapsed into the category of autonomous human power, regardless of the subjective understanding of political authorities themselves. In Luther's political thought about the two kingdoms or governments the secular state is the means by which God rules the fallen world by his left hand.

Whether this kind of Lutheran two-realm (or, more properly, dual-vocation) political theory can readily be applied to Islamic practice (which the fourth khalifa appears to do) is problematic given orthodox Islam's much fuller social blueprint as disclosed by God. Moreover "absolute justice" is not as objective and universal as the present Supreme Head optimistically thinks. As indicated in debates on abortion, homosexual rights, or the right to self-determination of the aboriginal people in Canada, it is not always transparent what the entailments of justice are. Much as many of us would like to believe in the possibility of a universal natural law that would enable us to handle the problems of justice and morality and peace across cultural and religious boundaries, it is not self-evident that such a natural law, universal in understanding and application, is available to us.

The question needs to be addressed whether the khalifa's teaching on the Islamic state does not result in an uncharacteristic truncation of Islamic social practice. In *Islam's Response to Contemporary Issues* (p. 197) Mirza Tahir Ahmad says, "A believer of any religion can practise his beliefs even under a secular law, he can abide by truth without any state law interfering with his ability to *speak* the truth. He can observe his prayers and perform his acts of worship without the need of a specific law being passed by the state to permit him to do so" (my emphasis).

Is this expression consistent with the distinctly this-worldly empirical thrust of Islam, which would insist not only on speaking the truth but on doing it by implementing the divinely revealed law for all of society? In exploring this problem Peggy and I spent two hours with Nasir, the principal of Jamia College. I shared with him certain reservations I have about Hazoor's way of formulating the Islamic conception of the state. His response was based, first of all, on the Qur'anic verse, "There is no compulsion in religion," which he took to be a mandate for the secular state. I had previously interpreted this verse to mean that one can never force conversion upon another. The principal took it to mean that even the individual duties enjoined by religion cannot be forced upon another. In this interpretation, secularism is seen as a positive force – a tolerant social structure that accommodates diverse religious and cultural groups. This comes close to the construction put upon secularism by Anas Ahmad, son of the third khalifa Mirza Nasir Ahmad, in an earlier interview, where the term secularism was just another way of expressing one's convictions about the values of a tolerant society.

But then there was a shift in the meaning of secularism where it was seen negatively as a competing worldview and value system that tends to impose its values on religious devotees with divergent values. This type of secular state facilitates or even imposes abortion, or enforces the employment of homosexuals in institutions like schools from which one might on religious principles wish to bar them. It was interesting to note that the principal functioned with a view of secularization as a religion in the way I customarily do on the basis of my generic definition of religion as a symbol system that induces and expresses the participants' selfhood in virtue of the symbols' communication of a world view and value system. On this wide definition many forms of secular tradition qualify as religion.

I suggested that secularism's fundamental social principle, at least in the Western liberal democracies, is individual liberty, which exists in a kind of elective affinity with a this-worldly naturalistic metaphysic. All citizens have the right of individual self-expression where it does not interfere with the similar expression of others. I am of the opinion that the Ahmadi interpretation of the Islamic state outlined above glosses the possibility of stark and irreconcilable value conflicts among groups. The principal suggested that if the secular state is prepared to enforce upon him the requirement that homosexuals not be excluded from employment in the educational institutions that he controls, that same secular state ought not to prohibit his exercise of the right of polygamy. I replied that in the interest of consistency, the liberal democratic secular state would have to allow him the individual right to polygamy if it could be reasonably argued that the practice does not infringe the rights of other citizens within the polity.

When I persisted with the possibility of the secular state's imposing standards of conduct that vitiate the rights of citizens to individual freedom where this is seen to infringe the corresponding right of others, the reply by Muhammad Ali, the principal's colleague, was that if such inexpungeable conflicts of value and conduct did emerge, Ahmadi Muslims would be faced with the choice either of working to change such legislation or migrating. This assumes the right of free movement for people who no longer wish to live in a state that prevents the free expression of their religion.

In discussing the question of religion and secularization, a curiously Protestant type of political theory emerged, reminiscent of Billy Graham's belief in the possibility of social transformation only through initial individual regeneration. The Graham view was that people needed first to get right with God, and then out of the converted heart would spring the proper moral attitudes and conduct that would rectify problems of race, industrial strife, international relations, and so on. A good tree brings forth good fruit. Anas Ahmad, for example, insisted that in Islam there can be no imposition of a social order through the state because Muslim behaviour flows only from an internal commitment. Only a person who has resolved to submit, to surrender, to God's revelation through the Prophet Muhammad as that revelation is exposited and interpreted through the Promised Messiah can hope to adopt Muslim behaviour. Such behaviour is not enjoined upon others because they do not have the necessary precondition of conversion and surrender that alone makes such behaviour intelligible and possible.

To reiterate, however, this particular approach seems to work only so long as one restricts the mandatory behaviour to what we might call religious duties, duties owing to God in the narrow sense of piety and worship. So long as one is speaking, for example, only of personal ritual behaviours such as *hajj* (pilgrimage), or wearing the veil, or fulfilling the fast, there is no particular problem in espousing this view. As I've noted elsewhere, our Ahmadi friends appear to be quite accepting of Peggy's going around without a veil and sometimes without covering her head. Because she is not a Muslim they don't expect from her the same degree of covering that they feel is mandatory for women fully participant in the Muslim community.

But once one moves to broader social issues outside the realm of such private duties as head covering, wearing the veil, and mandatory prayer and fasting during the month of Ramadan, then the problem becomes more acute. We do not, to take a transparent example, declare that ritual murder is optional depending upon one's religious presuppositions. Most societies have made the judgment that murder of the innocent is in all cases wrong, that it is to be prevented through coercive sanctions, and that where it is committed it should draw severe penalties.

What the Ahmadis call secularism, in a positive sense, as a hospitable framework for the tolerance of all religions, seems to be a blend of millet system and natural law. According to the millet system of the Turkish empire, communities like the Armenian Christian, Greek Orthodox, Roman Catholic, or various groups of Muslims or Jews could administer their religious laws inside their own communities relatively free of regulation by the central Turkish authorities. But when one moved from issues of personal status such as marriage, divorce, and inheritance to broader social issues like theft and violence and the keeping of contracts, then the universal imperial law, applicable to all regardless of their communitarian allegiance, came into force. The khalifa's reliance on the concept of absolute justice to regulate these broader affairs – a set of norms and values that are held even by a just secular state – displays his confidence in the existence of a universally persuasive natural law.

I have a certain feeling for the Jama'at-i-Islami, the orthodox group founded by Mawdoodi who are arch-opponents of the Ahmadis. The Jama'at-i-Islami viewpoint is certainly not my idea of an ideal political theory and I am indeed opposed to it, but I sympathize with it as a reflection of an Islamic stance on life. This orthodox group feels that it has a blueprint revealed by God for the totality of society and all its realms. An Islamic way of life in conformity with the divine will will come about only when Islamic society and eventually the world conforms to this shari'a, or divine blueprint for the totality of life. So long as religious duties are conceived of as the performance of pilgrimage or the five daily prayers or the giving of *zakat* (alms) or fasting, then no major problems emerge. Those who are Muslim can follow their conscience and perform these religious duties while those who are not will not fast during this period. The problem, to repeat, emerges with particular acuteness when we broaden our perspective to that of wider economic and social and political activity such as the rights of ethnic and cultural communities, the conduct of international relations, including warfare, and free-trade agreements or GATT negotiations in the economic sphere. Muslims represented by the Jama'at-i-Islami perspective contend that the divine will applies to these other spheres as well, which in liberal democratic societies are viewed as falling outside the hegemony of religion, instead pertaining either to an agreed-upon natural law typically expressed as human rights, or to a negotiated consensus amongst citizens with diverse interests.

The compromise that has been achieved in most secularized liberal societies is predicated on the universal value of freedom. The social contract that has been worked out holds that the maximum freedom should be allowed to all individuals and groups so long as these do not infringe upon the right of other individuals and groups to exercise their freedom. Take, for example, the issue of pornography. In an ideal Islamic society, pornography would be forbidden by law and there would be penalties attached to attempts to produce or distribute pornographic material. The consensus that seems to be emerging in liberal secular societies is that, regardless of one's own personal antipathy towards pornography, one is not permitted to infringe the right of those who wish to use pornography. Similarly with prostitution. Nasir agreed that an Islamic society would ideally prohibit, with the appropriate legal and penal sanctions, the practice of prostitution. I pointed out that in our own Canadian society, prostitution is no longer considered a crime, although soliciting is. With instances like these one can see the problem emerging where an Islamic perspective on life and an application of Muslim values is no longer just a matter of personal or communal allegiance and practice but spills over into wider social dimensions where agreement disappears. The khalifa's recourse to the principle of absolute justice is not as decisive as one might hope given the lack of consensus on the definition of absolute justice. Some might conclude that the application of absolute justice requires the taking of life for life; they might therefore support the death sentence for murder, whereas others might argue, also on the basis of their perception of absolute justice, that not even murder should be requited with the death penalty.

My own enunciated political theory, nevertheless, comes close in many respects to the khalifa's, in that I recognize that any other alternative is untenable in secularized and pluralistic societies. I do, however, raise the question to what extent other Muslims would accept that view as an authentic Islamic one. That is why I said that I had certain sympathies with the Jama'at-i-Islami, not because I view it as a cogent social program and political theory for an increasingly global and interconnected world, but because I understand how it can be promulgated as an intelligible and authentic Islamic perspective on society notwithstanding that it cannot be implemented.

Pluralism and the Islamic State

Mirza Anas Ahmad informed me that after the hijra Muhammad issued a letter to the Jews, the population in Madinah at that time being composed of Jews and Muslims, the pagans having accepted Islam. Muhammad said the Jews and Muslims were one *umma* – one community – and that therefore their rights were equal. Jews were free to practise their religion and Muslims were free to pursue their own. Those who committed crimes would be punished according to the sanctions prescribed by their own community; Jews according to Jewish law and Muslims according to Muslim law. If God had not disclosed an appropriate punishment for a crime, then at that stage in Islam's revelatory development, the Muslims would administer a punishment according to the Torah.

When we restrict our attention to religion, understood as the practice of the rituals and other acts of piety, there is generally speaking little problem. The more acute problem emerges, once again, on the level of civil behaviour and public crime. To say that the toleration within the Muslim *umma* in the Prophet's time permitted punishment of crimes according to the prescriptions of the respective communities begs the question what constitutes a crime. The definition of crime is not automatically a matter of cross-cultural agreement. Though we many discern consensus on some broad moral principles, the definitions of acts that constitute crimes against the community are variable. Thus, we are confronted with the problem of how a community composed of diverse religious traditions is to arrive at social concord in the absence of an agreement on what constitutes a crime. It may well be that the Medina of the Prophet's time did not present an acute problem inasmuch as the significantly shared world views and value systems of Jews and Muslims facilitated a degree of unanimity on crimes and their punishment.

I sensed that Anas had a much more sanguine view of the problems raised by religious and cultural diversity. Perhaps it is because of my greater awareness of the erosion of conventional religious traditions by the powerful emergent tradition of secularism that I am more attuned to the antagonisms that can emerge between communities with competing world views and values. Canada, a relatively tranquil country, is beset by enormous tensions in public life when social policies focus on questions raised by abortion, euthanasia, homosexuality, and the justice system. Different religious groups have different assessments of these practices as do secularized citizens.

Anas made a virtue of necessity by citing the Qur'an to the effect that not everyone agrees in this life: "Diversity of opinion among my followers is a blessing." Anas contemplates a synergistic relationship between diversity and harmony within a society, failing to grasp sufficiently the social animosity caused by religious diversity. I pressed the point that failing some *consensus gentium* about a natural and therefore universal moral law, we are left with damaging conflicts of moral principle and social policy, as when Canadian schoolboards obliged Muslim girls to abandon *hijab*, or head covering, on the grounds that it was prejudicial to the creation of a shared ethos within society. France's prohibition of *hijab* in state schools has become a paradigm instance of the conflict between secular state policy and particular religious practice. Anas acknowledged the reality of value conflicts amongst groups in a pluralistic society. The Qur'an, he pointed out, forbids usury, or the taking of interest. Nevertheless, the Promised Messiah declared that, in today's world, Muslims do not commit a sin when the practice of usury is forced upon them in order to survive economically – a legitimate compromise that deflects from the ideal but does not exclude one from the household of Islam. Likewise, the Qur'an declares that if one's survival is at stake and pork is the only available food, Muslims may eat the otherwise forbidden meat. Similarly, where the practice of purdah is impossible because of external pressures and the alternative is damage or destruction to individuals and the community, then the divine law can be suspended in the interest of survival.

This strategy of compromise is necessitated by the only other alternative open to Muslims when they are confronted with a civil law that violates their sense of the Qur'anic ideal. They are enjoined to obey the law of the land and if doing so is morally impossible they are obliged to emigrate. Where this policy of emigration would be impossible, then the solution of justifiable compromise emerges. What is not compromisable is faith in the unity of God and the Prophethood of Muhammad and, for Ahmadis, the Promised Messiah. Fidelity to these fundamental convictions means martyrdom is demanded before denial or compromise.

This particular view seems to resemble that of orthodox Judaism, which says that all laws can be violated in order to save life other than the law affirming the oneness of God and the law against murder or the killing of the innocent.

In support of this position that law is made for man and not man for the law, Anas quoted the Hadith of someone who approached the Prophet saying that he had violated the Ramadan fast by having sex with his wife during the forbidden period. The normal rule is that if one intentionally breaks the fast one is obliged to compensate or atone by fasting for sixty days – twice the prescribed fast time – or, alternatively, by giving alms to sixty poor persons. The supplicant asked the Prophet how, if he was unable to deny himself his sexual pleasure once, he could then deny himself sixty times, whereupon the Prophet said he should give to the poor. On responding that he had no money to do so, the Prophet produced a huge pail of dates, but the man reminded the Prophet that he was a poor man and that the food might better be used to feed his own children, whereupon the Prophet said that he should take the dates and go to his own family. This flexible, generous, compromisory attitude, Anas said, though it cannot be generalized into a law, indicates that the Qur'anic prescriptions are not inflexible apart from the ones mentioned; instead they are adaptable according to external circumstances. In the background of much of the Ahmadis' response to my concerns about ethics and social policy is their underlying confidence that these questions will become largely irrelevant as the ongoing march of Ahmadi Islam brings about the conversion of the whole world and, therefore, a shared commitment to the values and laws of Islam that will make discussion of conflict, contradiction, and compromise irrelevant.

As noted earlier, part of the problem with these discussions is the lack of agreement on the use of terms. For Anas Ahmad, Islam is the most modern of religions because it anticipates some of the most recent discoveries in evolutionary theory and genetics and even space travel. "Modern," to my Ahmadi informants, means contemporary scientific knowledge and technology, not a secular naturalistic social and psychological ethos.

Secularism as Tolerance

In speaking of the relation of Islam to secular society, Mirza Anas Ahmad made the astonishing claim that Islam created the first secular society. For evidence he harked back to the Jewish population in Madinah who were not obliged to subscribe to specifically Islamic law. They were expected to organize their society and moral lives according to Torah. From this Anas extrapolated the conclusion that Islam is addressed, in the first place, to individuals. What is required of persons who hear the preaching of Islam is to experience a conversion of the heart that prompts them to submit their lives to the will of God and to fulfill Islamic ordinances. Non-Muslims are not expected to adhere to a way of life that applies only to those lives who have been reoriented by turning to Islam.

Religious pluralism, that is to say the presence of both Muslim and Jewish communities in Madinah, was taken by Anas to signify a secular structure in which a multiplicity of faith claims are allowed to exist. This insistence on the primacy of the individual and the individual's internal conversion to God and Islam struck me as highly idiosyncratic – at least contrary to the usual way in which I have tried to explicate Islam by demonstrating its resolutely social character. Islam, unlike some brands of Christian or Buddhist piety, insists that the totality of human life, in all its dimensions including the political and economic, must be brought under the sovereignty of God. God the Creator has a divine blueprint, a masterplan, according to which a human life will be lived truly and morally if it conforms to that divine scheme. This is not an orientation that stresses the relativity of moral and social behaviour to specific and diverse forms of religious loyalty; rather it perceives that there is an intrinsic structure to reality that prescribes the right way for all persons to live if they but knew it. Islam is the revelation from God of that right way that conforms to the inherent nature of reality.

It is true, of course, that Muhammad recognized that Christians and Jews were recipients of a revelation and a book but those communities existed in relationship to their own prophets, especially Abraham, Moses, and Jesus. Though they had a certain continuing legitimacy, these communities, the recipients of an originally pure revelation from God, had perverted their scriptures so that they existed with an incorrect and deformed version of God's original truth and way of life. Thus, it is misleading to suggest that Islam proposed a secular structure that was neutral to all religious truth and morality claims. Rather, Islam promulgated an ideal divinely disclosed moral structure that Muslims acknowledged and attempted to implement. Within that framework, Christians and Jews were accorded a legitimacy that was only partial and qualified. This is not what we normally mean by a secular social framework. Instead it is an Islamic one that accords a qualified generosity towards other positions, mainly the Christian and Jewish ones. Muslim reservations about these other traditions were disclosed in the fact that Christians and Jews were, within an Islamic society, required to pay the poll tax, or *jizya*.

In the Ahmadi case this pluralist generosity is extended to other traditions like the Hindu and Buddhist – all of which are seen as fulfilled by the Promised Messiah. It is historically very misleading to characterize the pluralistic state of affairs depicted by Anas Ahmad in the early Madinah (which in his judgment is normative for Islam) as a secular state. The normative meaning of secular is a state of consciousness and a social arrangement in which there is no acknowledgment of the claims of religion in shaping both forms of thought and forms of society. Once again, while religious traditions may continue to exist, they do so largely as private affairs of piety or personal morality and not as inspiration to social legislation, this being arrived at instead by non-religious rational calculation. While it is true that one of the hallmarks of the secularization of society has been toleration of dissenting views so long as they do not threaten the fundamental secular contract, secularization cannot be equated with toleration.

What we appear to have in the Madinah of the Prophet is a pluralistic society that is allowed to flourish under the hegemony of an overarching Islamic social structure. This can hardly be called a secular state.

A common conceit (in which I have all too frequently indulged in the past) is that Islam, unlike Christianity, does not tolerate a division between the sacred and the secular, between the spiritual and the temporal, but rather operates with a divinely revealed law that pertains to the totality of human existence and all its spheres. An illustration of this integralist Islamic view may be found in the thought of Muhammad Rashid Reda (1865–1935), a scholar who did much of his work in Cairo. In advancing his vision of Islam as a totalistic way of life, he critiqued a contemporary of his who argued "that Islam has no Khalifa nor Imam nor government nor political or judicial legislation; it is a purely spiritual religion like Christianity as understood by the Protestant sect."

Here Protestant Christianity is portrayed as a "purely spiritual" religion devoted to the cultivation of inward spiritual states of devotion to the Lord Jesus to the exclusion of preoccupation with the temporal realm of politics, commerce, and economics. But this is a notion that I can scarcely recognize in any Protestant circles in which I have moved. It may characterize some sects of Christianity such as Pentecostals or other fundamentalist sects (although in recent times there has been a movement towards political hegemony even amongst American fundamentalists). The mainline Protestant churches have almost without exception embraced, to a greater or lesser degree, a comprehensive vocation for the Church that supplements its evangelistic and worship role with that of social and political witness. The United Church of Canada, most notably, combined these two vocations in one of its most powerful church boards, Evangelism and Social Service. Social Service included political testimony intended to shape government policy in a moral direction in conformity with Christian principles. To use Richard Niebuhr's typology, very few Protestant churches and certainly not the mainline denominations could be characterized as "Christ against culture." More typically, they exhibited the types termed by Niebuhr as "Christ of culture" in the churches' more liberal phases, or more typically the type of "Christ transforming culture." In either case the allegation that Protestant Christianity is concerned exclusively with a spiritual vocation to the exclusion of the temporal realm of politics and economics simply does not correspond to the facts.

God and Caesar: A Summary

We may discern three categories that attempt in their various ways to deal with the question of the relationship of God to the political realm. At one extreme end of the spectrum lies the theocratic view that there is a specific religious revelation of temporal laws that gives concrete instructions on how persons are to behave to conform to the will of God. Islamic jurisprudence, for example, contains specific guidance on whom one is allowed to marry by setting out the prohibited relationships that limit one's choice of spouse. This apodictic morality may be softened somewhat by acknowledging that in addition to quite specific commands disclosed in the Qur'an and in the Sunna of the Prophet, it is rationally possible to infer guides to action for situations that are analogous to those in the Qur'an for which there is a specific rule. This analogical reasoning, or *qiyas*, is given different weight in different schools of law ranging from its rejection in the Hanbali to its varying degree of authority in the remaining three schools. In any case, the main thrust of this point of view is that

God guides temporal matters and political obligations of everyday life by way of specific rules that have divine sanction.

At the other extreme of the spectrum is the dualistic view that the temporal or secular life is religiously irrelevant, the purpose of religion being to prepare the soul for a life of intimacy with God in this present life and thereafter for all eternity in Paradise. The secular realm of the state is allowed to run according to the autonomous principles of human reason and power and accommodation at work in secular life.

In between lies the view that there is a general divine sovereignty over temporal matters since only through this can the kingship of God over the whole of creation be affirmed. The specific forms of that divine sovereignty, however, are not spelled out in detail in revelation but, rather, have to be extrapolated from very general principles of social morality. So, for example, though God commands justice as the general principle for social intercourse, the specific form that justice assumes in a particular social situation of competing interests is something that has to be arrived at by human calculation. A religiously stronger version of this point of view argues that although there is no explicit divine revelation of social and political rules (at least not comprehensively so), the exercise of human rationality and will in the temporal realm in order to serve the divine demands of justice amounts to an act of religious obedience. The secular in a sense becomes the sacred. To repeat the Lutheran formulation of this perspective, the secular realm with its intrinsic principles of justice and power – social order backed up by punitive sanctions – is not an autonomous realm of human activity divorced from divine initiative but is rather the means by which God rules the temporal realm with his left hand.

The Ahmadi position in this tripartite typology occupies the middle area between theocracy and autonomy. I do not think the Lutheran comparison is an unacceptable stretch. Just as Luther declared that the Turks (the Muslims with whom he was acquainted) could be better civil rulers than many Christian princes, so the Ahmadi khalifa holds that non-Muslim secular authorities do their divinely appointed work when they govern with justice in maintaining civil order and protecting the nation.

This conception of religion and politics satisfies the theological requirement to acknowledge God's sovereignty while at the same time remaining flexible to the situational demands and rational calculations of pluralistic and secular societies.

CHAPTER SIX

Harassment and Persecution

The amir of Sargoda, who is also the amir of Punjab province, is an incredibly alert and vital ninety-five-year-old. Mirzah Abdul Haq is the father of thirteen children, three of whom died in childhood; of the ten surviving children, one died at age sixty-seven just a few days before my interview with him. The amir was dressed in a cream-coloured *shalwar kameez* and a long frock coat identical to the type worn by the second khalifa, as well as a white Punjabi turban with the starched plume extending from the top. He met the second khalifa in 1913 when he was thirteen years old. A spiritually sensitive boy, he was immediately drawn to the khalifa and his teachings. In 1916 he was converted and made *bai'at* to the khalifa. In 1917 he began to wear a *shalwar* long frock coat as did the khalifa and sported the characteristic Ahmadi beard, practices that were then frowned upon in the Indian civil service, which he had joined in 1918. He married his first wife at age twenty-three. Three years later in 1926, in response to an order by the khalifa, he left the civil service and began a private law practice at Gudaspur. There he married his second wife, the widow of an uncle of his. He felt it was his responsibility to assume the role of caretaker and protector for her and her three children, though he conceded that she was also a beautiful woman. In response to Peggy's question he acknowledged that his first wife, to whom he had only been married for three years, had initially shown some resistance to the match. The second marriage, however, was not the result of consultation with the first wife but rather the announcement of an intention he had already reached.

To this day the amir recites the Qur'an at least one hour every day. Since 1918 he has never missed a single one of the five daily obligatory prayers, nor has he missed a fast since 1918 and he is still fasting even though his age exempts him. For most of his life he has observed the *tahajud*, which entails rising at two in the morning and then praying for up to two or three hours, the average being about one and a half hours. It is his conviction that the *tahajud* prayer is especially effective in beseeching God's pardon for one's faults. When he was forty he had a dream in which God announced to him that he would take even better care of him in the future than he had in the past. He has scarcely ever been ill and money has come to him from many sources even when he has not worked. He lives alone on the family compound, although several of his children live nearby and he takes his meals with one of his daughters since his wife died at age eighty-seven, a few years ago. His second wife died at age seventy-five.

A couple of episodes in the amir's life highlight the quandary in which Ahmadis are placed as they seek to participate in the civil life of their society without at the same time relinquishing their self-identity as Muslims. The amir was offered a position as advisor on minorities to the Pakistani president in 1980 on the condition that he would acknowledge that he was himself a member of one of the minorities. But to do so would be tantamount to admitting that he was not a Muslim, given the 1974 constitutional amendment declaring the Ahmadis to be a non-Muslim religious minority. This condition he could not accept. He declared: I am a Muslim, I testify to the existence and unity of God, I offer the obligatory prayers, I believe in the prophet of God, I believe in the sanctity of the Qur'an, and I performed the hajj in 1972 before Ahmadis were refused visas to travel to Saudi Arabia. In addition to these basic Muslim tenets, he professed his belief in the truthfulness of the Promised Messiah. Around the same time, he was offered a position on the Majlis *shura*, or the National Assembly, as the official representative of the Ahmadis, certain seats being set aside for minorities. This he also felt he had to refuse, for the same reason. Shortly thereafter he received from Islamabad an unsigned letter asking why his estate should not be confiscated since he refused to sit in the National Assembly as a representative of the Ahmadi minority and refused even to enter his name on the minority voting list. His reaction to this harassment was characteristic of most Ahmadis – even trials are not a contradiction of their confidence in God's mercy, providence and care but are seen as divine initiatives by which He tests his people and causes their character to grow.

Legislative Persecution

Within Pakistan the Ahmadis have long been persecuted through the laws, the courts, and the prejudice of their fellow Muslims. The collision between Ahmadi piety and political expediency is another manifestation of the uneasy fit between religious tradition and secular modernity.

In 1974, during the tenure of Zulfikar Ali Bhutto, the Ahmadis were declared by constitutional amendment to be a non-Muslim minority, despite their self-definition as Muslims. Ten years later the anti-Ahmadi Ordinance No. 20 of 1984 was introduced into the Pakistani criminal code by Zia-ul-Haq, who had also ordered the hanging of Bhutto. Ordinance No. 20 and especially its article 298C made it possible to prosecute Ahmadis on a charge of posing to be a Muslim, which carried a sentence of three years imprisonment. The blasphemy laws of 1993, introduced by then prime minister Nawas Sharif, intensified religious persecution by carrying a penalty of death for blaspheming the name of the Prophet. The context at the time was the famous Salman Rushdie affair precipitated by his novel *The Satanic Verses*. The worldwide Muslim indignation at what they saw as Rushdie's impugning of the reputation and moral and spiritual status of the Prophet was reflected in Pakistan by the introduction of the 1993 law. The question I raised was what specific interests would prompt Nawas Sharif to introduce such a law.

In his campaign for election Nawas Sharif had promised the Islamic clerics and their supporters that he would introduce comprehensive shari'a law as he moved Pakistan towards thoroughly Islamic statehood. This of course he could not do for economic and political reasons. The abolition of the traditional banking and interest system in favour of Islamic shared venture capitalism (where the taking of interest is regarded as a sin) would have shipwrecked the Pakistani economy in the global context. Consequently, in order to appease the extremist mullahs, he introduced the blasphemy laws, which cost him very little politically apart from some international condemnation. It did not alienate the powerful Pakistan economic ruling class, whose interests would have been shattered by the introduction of shari'a law, particularly at the economic level. The blasphemy law allowed the government to appear pious before the Islamist mullahs and the congregations that they control through their Friday sermon and preaching venues, while at the same time limiting any political damage to Sharif himself.

Some cases were brought against Christians under the blasphemy laws and two or three cases were still pending during the time of our stay in 1995. The Ahmadi leadership believed, however, that a directive had gone out from the government that no further Christians were to be prosecuted under the law, for during most of 1994 no Christians had been charged with blasphemy in spite of the view of some Christians that Muhammad is a demonic and fraudulent imposter. The Ahmadis remain, as they were always intended to be, the primary target of this legislation.

Naseen Saifi is editor of the *Al Fazl Daily*, the Ahmadi paper founded in 1913 by the second khalifa and published out of Rabwah. It has published continuously except during 1984–88, when it was banned by government decree. It resumed publication in 1988 after the regulations changed.

Saifi is an energetic seventy-eight-year-old who belies the fact that he spent thirty-one days in jail in 1994, incarcerated with dacoits (armed bandits) and heroin users and dealers. Forty people were crammed into a cell that was just large enough to provide space to lie down. He was charged originally under article 298c of the penal code, which penalizes those who are posing as Muslims. To this the judge added 295c, the crime of blasphemy against the Prophet, which carries the death penalty. This charge was based on the newspaper's having referred to the khalifa as Hazoor, a term the judge deemed appropriate only with respect to the Prophet. In fact, as Saifi pointed out, Hazoor is a common term of respect in Pakistan. At the railway station the taxi wallahs will call to you, "Hazoor, you need a taxi, a taxi for Hazoor." One can see how flimsy are the grounds and how vehement the efforts to intimidate the Ahmadis and frustrate their missionary outreach. At seventy-seven years of age Saifi spent the month of February in arduous prison conditions, but he regards it as a blessing from God that he was found worthy of suffering some inconvenience in pursuit of obedience to God and Islam. He laughed heartily when I told him that one of my favourite sermons in the days when I was a preacher was entitled "The Lost Christian Art of Going to Jail," which took as its text Paul's catalogue of the sufferings, including a series of incarcerations, he had endured in pursuing his calling to spread the Gospel.

Saifi still has forty-five court cases pending against him. His own judgment is that the court is stalling in the prosecution of these cases, caught between the obligation to punish him on the basis of the existing lunatic anti-Ahmadi legislation on the one hand, and, on the other, the wrath of the mullahs should they decline to do so.

Pakistan appears to be increasingly in a state of social unrest not only in Sind, and especially Karachi and Baluchistan, but spreading up into the Punjab and the Northwest Frontier. There are mounting Sunni-Shi'a tensions and conflicts and the supposition is that the Sunnis are supported by Saudi Arabia and the Shi'a by Iran. In this situation *Al Fazl* cannot distribute by mail because a number of copies have been seized and destroyed so now they rely mainly on hand-couriering of bundles of papers to the outlying communities.

Passport applications constitute another form of harassment to Ahmadis. Those applying for a passport are required to indicate what religion they belong to. If they indicate Muslim then they have to testify to clauses in which they declare Mirza Ghulam Ahmad to be an imposter prophet. In other words, to assert one's identity as an adherent of a particular religion, one must condemn and nullify another religion. Of course the Ahmadis cannot sign such a declaration, so most of them apply as Ahmadis, which means they apply as a minority, which entails a de facto repudiation of their self-identity as Muslims. The religion that appears on their passports is Ahmadi instead of Muslim. The presence of the clauses on the passport application requiring Muslims to denounce Mirza Ghulam Ahmad is not the result of legislation but is an administrative directive and could thus be removed by government fiat. In spite of the embarrassment the government faces internationally in human rights forums, it has so far been disinclined to remove the clauses because of the alliance of interest that it has made with certain of the mullah class and their supporters.

The Ahmadis ask why a citizen's religious identity should appear on the passport in the first place and view it as a contrivance to intimidate and confuse them. The analogy that Nasrullah Khan uses is to imagine a country with a predominantly Christian population requiring its citizens, when applying for a passport, to indicate that their identity as Christians entails their repudiation of another religious tradition. To affirm my Christianess, for example, I might be obliged by the state to assert that Judaism is a false, obsolete, and superseded religion. This conveys the flavour of the Ahmadi umbrage at analogous clauses in the Pakistan passport application.

Political Manipulation of the Courts

The courts provide another venue for the harassment and persecution of Ahmadis. Returning to the example of the blasphemy laws, the government of Pakistan, under pressure from Western diplomats, explained in 1995 that it was not able to change the blasphemy law at the time because of political pressures but that it would deal with the law by way of a directive that there should be a judicial inquiry before a First Information Report, or FIR, was filed with the police. In theory, the directive would put the brakes on malicious or frivolous applications of a poorly defined law that carried the death penalty. In fact the directive appears to have had no effect. A case in point was in Rajanpur. A group of mullahs went to the house of the amir of the local *jama'at* and hammered at his gate, demanding to enter into a religious dialogue. This was a ruse to get the amir to promulgate Ahmadi doctrine. The amir refused, saying that

Ahmadis were not allowed by the law to preach. Realizing that their ruse had failed, the mullahs went to the police station and complained that the amir had abused the Prophet Muhammad and was therefore liable to the death sentence under the blasphemy laws. As required by the directive from the Ministry of Law and Justice, a judicial inquiry by a magistrate was held and the result was the dismissal of the accusations by the mullahs. A second judicial inquiry also led to the dismissal of the charges against the amir. Nevertheless, the local deputy commissioner insisted that the charges should be proceeded with. This means that the softening of the blasphemy laws by the Ministry's directive was fictional rather than factual.

Sayed Kamarn Rizbi, adviser to the human rights cell of the Pakistan Ministry of Law and Justice, is a Shi'a who was jailed during Zia-ul-Haq's regime for distributing pamphlets against martial law. He was sentenced to thirty-five years in prison and served eight of them, partly in solitary confinement and partly in irons. He informed me that a human rights desk had been established within the Peoples' Party of Pakistan (PPP) in November 1990. When the PPP formed a government they established a desk of human rights within the Ministry of the Interior. In August of 1994, the desk was moved to the Ministry of Law and Justice where I was visiting him. Rizbi conceded that my concern about the Ahmadi situation was well placed and that the constitutional changes of 1974 were "unjust." No one is in a position to judge who is a Muslim and who is not, he said, thus affirming that it is outside the state's prerogative to define the Muslimness of Ahmadis. He attributed the persecution of the Ahmadis largely to "fanatic" groups in Pakistan deriving from the Zia era who had perpetrated attacks on Ahmadi families, but he explained that the election of the present government had brought change: "We are trying our level best to protect all Pakistani families from acts of violence and have also instructed the provincial governments to facilitate us and to arrest culprits of attacks on Ahmadis."

I alluded to the blasphemy trial then being conducted in Lahore against two Christians currently facing death sentences. Rizbi said, "we cannot say a problem is not there." Why, I asked, did the fundamentalists exercise such power over the political life of Pakistan, especially when the fundamentalist parties held only three or four seats in Parliament? Why did they hold sway over those who intimidate the government, Parliament, and the bureaucracy? Rizbi pointed to the capacity of the fundamentalist mullahs to get their Madrasa students out into the streets in large and turbulent numbers, many of them armed with lethal weapons. He described these students as barbaric fanatics who claimed to be protesting in the name of God and in defence of the honour of the Prophet.

Rizbi conveyed the notion that the attacks on Ahmadis are the consequence of mullah-inspired mob action. But I pointed out that the laws reinforce and encourage those acts of violence by giving political sanction to the harassment and persecution of Ahmadis. Moreover, Ahmadis have testified that in many instances the criminal court proceedings against them have been initiated by police officials themselves. Where not initiated by them, they have been acquiesced in by police officials in response to accusations by mullahs or their supporters that Muslim sensibilities have been outraged by Ahmadis uttering the *Bismillah* or reciting or portraying the *Kalimah*, or even using the greeting of *Assalam-o-alaikum*.

I emphasized this apparent government initiative and responsibility for the harassment of Ahmadis in order to pre-empt the government's disavowal of its complicity by attributing all acts of violence, harassment, and arson against Ahmadis either to hostile individuals or, alternatively, mob agitations instigated by fundamentalist mullahs. I conveyed my view that the existing legislation and administration served to create a climate in which the Ahmadis were fair game. Rizbi repeated that forthcoming changes in the law would alter the communal sanctions against the Ahmadis. The changes were being discussed amongst the national assembly coalition parties and would ease the legal and penal burdens against the Ahmadis. But he insisted throughout our talk that the government of Pakistan found itself in a very difficult position because of pressure and intimidation by what he described as the fanatical mullahs.

The interview with Rizbi was candid in acknowledging the depth and extent of the problem that is confronted by Ahmadis in present day Pakistan. But the spin remained optimistic that the necessary changes would be made in due course when the political and parliamentary situation permitted. After half an hour, he made clear moves that the interview should be brought to an end. Indeed, some ten minutes earlier, a female assistant who turned out to be his sister-in-law had come into his office with papers and sat down in the chair adjacent to mine, implying that there was business to be attended to.

There is a certain sadness about our moving around the compound and elsewhere throughout Rabwah. There are a number of large and attractive guesthouses that are not much used at this time. They were originally built in response to the revelation to the Promised Messiah that hospitality should be given to all the members of the community who assembled at the annual *Jalsa*, or assembly. Various institutions or subgroups within the Ahmadi organizational structure, such as the youth group, the women's group, the senior men's group, and the foreign missions office, have built their own guesthouses to accommodate their visitors. Ours is quite a fine one and has a number of rooms but we are the only occupants, partly because they wish to give us privacy but also because there isn't the demand that there once was. After Zia-ul-Haq's draconian Ordinance 20 of 1984, the *Jalsa* was forbidden and so for a decade now there has been no annual meeting in Rabwah, even though this institution, which involves the whole community, or as much of it as possible, coming together, was an integral part of Ahmadi practice.

Change and Violence

Over ninety-five percent of the population of Rabwah are Ahmadis. This accounts for the enormous feeling of security that we have there and helps to explain why so many Ahmadis like to settle in Rabwah. They not only feel spiritually close to their own kind but also experience a relative sense of security in Pakistan. We would be in danger of violence if mullah-agitated mobs, predominantly Madrasa (Islamic college) students, were to come in from outside to cause a disturbance in Rabwah. This has happened in the past: a gang of youth organized by the Jama'at-i-Islami came into the Rabwah railway station and offended some young Ahmadi girls, which caused the young Ahmadi men to retaliate in order to defend the honour of the community's womenfolk. We ourselves experienced a moment of unease one evening when Karim, who was visiting us at our bungalow, and the *chowkadar* became very concerned about four Turkish students who had appeared at the gate seeking an interview with us. This caused alarm, first of all because we did not know how these students could ever have known that Peggy and I were present at the Tahrik-i-Jadeed and also because these alleged students did not give any context in which they might have met us or learned of us. The Ahmadis immediately drew the inference that there was a possibility of mischief afoot. The "students" were sent away and we never did discover who they were or what they wanted.

Episodes of violence are extremely rare in Rabwah. But elsewhere in Pakistan innocent Ahmadis have been gunned down or knifed in the streets. In the months preceding our visit in 1995, an Ahmadi professor of physics in Islamabad was shot and killed when he opened his door to a knock in the evening. Earlier another professor at the Islamic university in Islamabad was knifed and killed, presumably by disgruntled fundamentalist students who felt he was not sufficiently conservative to suit their ideological bent. I was told by the missionary Naseer that the mullahs have preached that anyone who kills an Ahmadi will go directly to heaven, a special place being reserved for anyone who eliminates an Ahmadi from the face of the earth. In Sind a person was charged with the murder of an Ahmadi and when asked why he had done so, he replied that the mullah had told him that he had a heavenly destiny upon killing an Ahmadi. His trial was finally terminated on the grounds that he was not mentally competent and he was sentenced to the amount of time he had already spent in jail while awaiting trial.

Every day Ahmadis face an underlying animus that is intended to render their life difficult in whatever way lies at hand. They have to send their children to hostile schools. They work in situations where their advancement is limited by their loyalties to Ahmadiyyat and where they are in constant danger of unprovoked violence because of their religious profession. In medical schools the highly conservative student groups have taken it upon themselves to target Ahmadis. Dr Latif Qureshi's son and other Ahmadis in the medical college in Lahore were told that they were not wanted by the other students in the hostel dining-room because they were *kafirs* (unbelievers). The superintendent of the hostel, in order to obviate any problems, then had the Ahmadi students' meals served in their rooms, whereupon the conservative Sunni students charged that the Ahmadis were receiving privileged treatment and demanded that the favouritism, as they viewed it, cease.

Hamid Khan, the amir of the Lahore *jama'at*, reports that since 1984, the year of Ordinance 20, there have been sixty-four murders of Ahmadis in Pakistan and there has not been a single detainee in connection with any of these murders. From this they draw the inference, which seems logical enough, that there is no serious judicial attempt to bring the murderers of Ahmadis to justice. Driving with Hamid one day from Lahore to Rabwah, he told us what he knew of the murder of his thirty-four-year-old son in February 1994, the year before our visit. He was bludgeoned and stabbed to death in a little guesthouse on their large compound property. The investigation seems to have been extraordinarily sloppy, the authorities making scarcely any attempt to preserve forensic evidence. Hamid's view is that the murder was carried out by a group of Muslim students based at a particular medical college who were under the influence of a fundamentalist Islamic *pir*, or holy man. They have in recent years been abducting Ahmadi students, dragging them to the outskirts of the city, and beating them severely before abandoning them.

I might once have assumed that the social status and prestige of Hamid's family in Lahore society would have preserved them from this kind of brutal attack. In Pakistan family background, antiquity, and connection count for a great deal, or used to until the fairly recent encroachment of modernity with its levelling of social and historical particularities. Hamid's assumption is that it was precisely the prominence of his family that inspired the murder of his son, which sent an unequivocal message throughout the Ahmadi community that no one is safe from those militant Islamists who see themselves as the champions of Islamic authenticity and the Ahmadis as apostates from Islam who blaspheme the Prophet by suggesting that there was any type of prophecy after Muhammad.

The following anecdote, related to us by Hamid, shows the role the family connection played in Pakistan at one time. His father-in-law, Zafrulla Khan, was campaigning for office in the Sialkot area before universal suffrage had been introduced and certain leading figures or landowners were deputed to cast votes. Zafrulla Khan visited one very old man and asked for his vote. The old man's relatives tried to explain to him the identity of the candidate. Finally it emerged that Zafrulla Khan was the grandson of Sikander Khan, and once this had got through to the old man his mind was made up. "Give him the chit," he declared, meaning his vote. His sons interpolated, "But you promised to vote for the *pir*," to which the old man replied, "He comes once a year for a mound [a unit of measurement] of wheat and two rupees. If he doesn't come back, it doesn't matter." The point here is that many social and political decisions were made on the basis of loyalty to clan lineage and distinguished representatives of old families.

According to Idris Khan, Hamid's brother, with the dissolution of the close kinship ties that marked the earlier tribal societies of Pakistan, the Ahmadis have been put more at risk. In the old days when tribal, clan, and family ties were much more secure, the Ahmadis would be protected by their Sunni kinfolk who, even though they dissented from Ahmadi doctrine, would nevertheless say, "This is my third cousin, or that is my uncle, or this person is related to my sister's husband," and so on. This would be a natural restraint on acts of violence against Ahmadis. With the pressures of secular modernity (a term that I and not Idris introduced into the discussion), these ancient ancestral family groupings have been eroded as persons are more and more obliged to conform to the individual units of production and consumption required by modern capitalist industrial society. This dissolution of tribal loyalties has caused the Ahmadis to lose one of their more important sources of protection and security in the midst of a hostile Sunni environment.

The Government Speaks

When I phoned to arrange an interview in February 1995 with Lutfulla Mufti of the Pakistan Ministry of Religion and Minority Affairs in Islamabad, he surprised me by saying that I could come immediately. As I was ushered into his office I noted three deputies lined up in chairs in front of the minister's desk in the customary Pakistani fashion. One of these jumped up right away and gave me his chair. The minister was a handsome man with greying hair and an impressive self-presentation. He already knew from a fax I had sent from Canada that I was interested in social ethics and the impact of religious world views and value systems on social policy. Declaring my particular interest in the Ahmadi question, I did not tell him immediately that I had written a book on the subject, but I think he knew in the light of information that came out later.

He wanted to know my religious affiliation and I explained that I was an ordained clergyman in the United Church of Canada (of which he seemed to have heard) who had been recycled as an academic. He perplexed me by remarking: "I surmised that you are someone who has temporarily lost faith but has hope," a delicate way of suggesting that I was agnostic. I replied that while my orientations are, in fact, heavily secularist, I have a great regard and even nostalgia for religion because of the way it shapes human lives and has informed my own.

He continued to draw me out, wanting to know if I was married, and when I answered that I was, he urged me to go downstairs and get my wife. When I explained that I had dropped her off elsewhere, he said, "Oh that's too bad." He then apologized, saying, "You know we are in Ramadan, so we cannot entertain you at a meal right now, but I hope some evening this week you will be able to join us."

He then laid out his own religious position, insisting that he was just a simple man. Islam, he stated, has five basic beliefs: the existence and unity of God, the prophetic succession and the final prophet Muhammad, the Holy Books, the angels, and the Last Day. The first part of our meeting was given over to his own personal theology and interpretation of Islam. It seemed at times that he was trying to avoid the Ahmadi issue by restricting our exchange to talk about Islam as he understood it. He gave a highly demythologized interpretation of the angels as laws of nature. Then he talked about the prophetic succession and explained how Abraham was a great khalifa and other doctrinal points that are a standard introduction to Islam. He mentioned the liberal reformer Sayyid Ahmad Khan,[1] whose metaphorical interpretation of certain parts of the Qur'an – such as the ascension of Muhammad's Night of Journey – he endorsed. That he would be invoking a liberal modernizer as an authority seemed to me interesting, even contradictory. He then went on to explain that for Islam God is very potent. He sounded like a Sufi at this point, repeating that God is closer than the jugular vein. He articulated a baffling theology according to which the left atrium is considered to be the seat of the spirit of man. I remarked that Descartes found the soul's contact in the pineal gland, whereas he located the spirit in one of the atria of the heart.

This conversation reminded me of my visit a few days before to the Pakistan Tourist and Development Corporation to get some information about buses to Gilgit and Hunza. I never did find what I wanted to know. Instead I was treated to a sermon by the head of the section who began by telling me how erudite a scholar in comparative religion he was. He then laid out his understanding of the way the religions are related to one another. Judaism is the religion of justice and law; Christianity the religion of unconditional love. But since neither of these is sufficient to achieve a harmonious world, Islam was sent by God to integrate the compassion of Jesus and the law and justice of Abraham. I previously encountered in some Western scholars this way of perceiving the relationships among the biblical religions. I cannot imagine a Western bureaucrat digressing to an extended disquisition on theological matters.

Lutfulla Mufti, meanwhile, spent quite a bit of time talking about Iqbal,[2] whom he obviously admired. The minister used Iqbal to show

[1] Sayyid Ahmad Khan (1817–1898) was an Indian Muslim who founded Aligarh University, which incorporated Western social and natural sciences alongside the study of Qur'an and Hadith.

[2] Muhammad Iqbal (1887–1938) was a Muslim philosopher and poet who, as president of the Muslim League, advocated the creation of a separate Islamic state in northwest India. The influence on his thought of the vitalistic, voluntaristic, and process philosophies of Bergson, Nietzsche, and Whitehead may be seen in his *Reconstruction of Religious Thought in Islam* (1934).

that there had been a universal longing among religions for a promised deliverer and that the deliverer was Muhammad. He said there is no sanction in the Qur'an for the notion of the Messiah coming again. The belief, he explained may be found in folklore and in some of the most poorly attested hadiths.[3]

At that point there was a shift in the discussion. The minister asked whether I'd heard of a new book by Bashir Ahmed claiming a British Jewish connection to the Ahmadis. He mentioned an Alistair Lang, about whom I knew nothing and who claims that the accession of the Hindu maharaja of Kashmir to India after partition in 1947 (rather than to Pakistan as mandated by Kashmir's majority Muslim population) was never really signed. Some, including the Ahmadis, he continued, are responsible for promulgating the view that the accession to India was really signed. I said that whether or not accession was signed by the maharaja was irrelevant, the determining principle being the Muslim majority population and its right to self-determination. He conceded that that was true and then changed the subject, picking up the anachronistic idea that the Ahmadis were connected with the 1857 Mutiny, which is, for Indians, the war of independence. As the minister told it, the British were so discomfited by the mutiny that, in collusion with groups of Christian missionaries, they decided to divide the Muslim forces by creating or encouraging this notion of a Promised Messiah. They found someone in Qadian who would serve the purpose of fragmenting the Muslim forces. The minister asked, "Do you know what angel spoke to the (alleged) Promised Messiah?" He declared that the revelations were in English. I said that the majority were in Urdu and some were in Arabic, but he maintained that most of the Promised Messiah's revelations were in English. His intended message was that they had really been concocted by British agents.

Lutfulla Mufti conceded that at first Mirza Ghulam Ahmad had been a reformer and a pious man, but then he took most of this back. "We won't talk about his personal failings; after all, we are all human and we

---

[3] This is an overstated dismissal of the Muslim belief in the Messiah's return, though the minister had a point. The *Encyclopedia of Islam* asserts that the Qur'anic and Hadith allusions are few and obscure.

all have personal failings so we won't talk about his." I asked what kind of personal failings he meant. The minister explained that the Founder had boasted about his sexual prowess and graphically described his sexual adventures and also his venereal diseases. But such insinuations contradict the standard historical portrait of Mirza Ghulam Ahmad as an ascetic person with Sufi tendencies. Even if they were true, I asked, would they not simply make him a bad Muslim? Why was it necessary to drum him out of the whole Islamic faith? In the wake of the 1954 Munir Report on the Punjab disturbances of 1953, a consensus had emerged in Islam that the way Muslims deal with divisions of opinion is by the formula "He is a Muslim who says he is a Muslim." Whether he truly is a Muslim is left to divine judgment on the Last Day. Why, I queried, did the government escalate to the use of the mammoth and unwieldy legislation of Ordinance 20? The minister replied that the Ahmadis brought it on themselves.

It struck me that the Canadian High Commissioner, Marie-Andrée Beauchemin, when we visited her at the High Commission in Islamabad, had used the identical phrase in her meeting with us. Even at the time I thought that she was parroting some of the lines she had learned at dinner parties; the fault, she proposed, might be the rigidity of the Ahmadis themselves.

I mentioned my book *Conscience and Coercion* in which I had dealt with many of these issues. The minister asked whether it was available in the bookstores in Pakistan. I replied that I did not think so. Perhaps he was expecting me to disclose that the Ahmadis have it. I suggested that it may have been banned, but he assured me, "No we don't censor." I felt compelled to reveal that at the Anjuman I had been shown a list of many pages of censored books – more than four hundred publications have been banned by the government of Pakistan. Mainly this means that all export of Ahmadi books from Pakistan is prevented. *Conscience and Coercion* was not on the list but the list was a couple of years out of date, and it has been reported to us that the book has indeed been banned in Pakistan. He smiled and laughed. He returned to his previous objection, "Why do the Ahmadis insist on such an extreme and rigid attitude?" I replied that I could not be certain and asked what he thought the reason was. His answer: "The same reason as 1857." It struck me as bizarre that the Ahmadis were being connected with the Mutiny and the aftermath of 1857.

There was a discernible shift in the tenor of our exchange. The Ahmadis, he declared, had hijacked Islam. If they practised a religion of their own, that would be acceptable; instead they used epithets that appropriated orthodox Islam to their own duplicitous purposes. Why, for example, did they insist on calling the leader of their community khalifa, why didn't they just use their own terms? I reiterated that my focus was not the truth or falsehood of Ahmadiyyat but rather the right to self-definition. Unless one breaks the law in some way such as by killing or hurting someone, every person, whether we like them or not, should have the right to testify as to who they are, to their own definition of their faith, their own commitment and values.

I shared my view that the Ahmadis were very devout and their moral life upright: "Your praying is excessive, you're bothering God too much!" I tease my Ahmadi friends. The minister said that he knew their virtue because he too had Ahmadi friends and neighbours. Nevertheless, he argued, "Why do they insist on hijacking our religion?" But why consider it hijacking? The Ahmadis testify to the unity of God. The Promised Messiah's testimony to the Prophet Muhammad is full of veneration, praise, gratitude. These, I said, are the realities. They have their own self-perception as true Muslims, and if others disagree they should denounce Ahmadiyyat as bad Islam. But the Ahmadis should be allowed to say who they think they are.

The minister then objected to their method of preaching. The promulgation of their message is devious and masks their real intent; they pose as Muslims, he claimed, in the sense of impersonating Muslims. Ahmadi leaders do not let their commonfolk read the Promised Messiah's utterances: the verses are so bad that it would immediately be perceived what an imposter the Founder is. Bad as poetry or bad as theological content? I asked. To which the minister replied, both. The government operates with an unfalsifiable position. If someone asserts that the Ahmadi do indeed profess the five articles of Islamic faith, the official riposte is, maybe so, but they are dissimulating. There is no way of rebutting the government position, for no matter what the Ahmadis say, they are held to be lying or dissembling. The whole discussion starts with the assumption of bad faith and there is never any expectation that Ahmadis might be sincere. The real issue, said the minister, is internal subversion of Pakistan by means of Ahmadi dissimulation.

If all of this was true, I suggested, surely there were provisions in the penal system to deal with subversion. Why go to the bother of enacting legislation and changing the constitution in a manner aimed only at Ahmadis? At first the minister claimed that there have been only two or three charges brought against them. I argued that in fact there have been many and that I had documentation, many legal documents from Ahmadi charges and trials that I collected on my 1987 trip and thereafter.

I wanted him to understand that I am fond of Pakistan, that I had been there five times; that I enjoy the country and the culture and the Islamic way of family life. I wanted him to understand that I am not a hostile critic. Why, I asked, would Pakistanis embarrass themselves by their unjust treatment of a religious minority like the Ahmadis? Three times he repeated, "You are an innocent professor and I am a simple man and I know nothing about politics." We had been together over an hour. I thanked him, commenting that I had been expecting a ten-minute interview followed by a perfunctory bureaucratic dismissal, to which he responded that he was so glad I'd come and glad to have been able to chat. At the beginning of our interview he had suggested that we should have a couple of meetings but he did not bring this up again, nor was the dinner invitation renewed.

Cultural Integrity and Moral Absolutes

There is no need to play tolerant liberals who feel that cultural generosity obliges us to accept all sorts of peculiar behaviour that would contradict our own sense of moral rightness. In Canada, for example, we have decided that it is a crime to perform clitoridectomies or other forms of genital mutilation on young girls and women regardless of the cultural mandate to do so in their countries of origin. Cultural particularities, it is contended, must be subordinated to our perception of moral law. Pakistan is not our country; nevertheless we can use an analogous type of reasoning to appeal to universal principles of human decency that stand in judgment upon the Pakistan government's treatment of Ahmadis. The fact that such universal principles do exist in spite of genuine and wide-ranging cultural diversity is evidenced by theoretical agreement to the Universal Declaration of Human Rights, which Pakistan has signed.

Although our ability to interfere in the internal affairs of another country is severely limited, that does not require that we remain totally mute. At the very least we can prevent the violators of elementary human rights from performing their deeds in darkness. A relevant biblical text might well be "The light has come into the world and men love the darkness because their deeds are evil." At the very least we must embarrass the perpetrators of these judicial injustices against a religious community like the Ahmadi.

There is also the possibility of exercising censure and encouraging movement towards change by insisting on tied aid. Canada is still a substantial donor of aid to Pakistan, though mainly through the work of non-governmental organizations, or NGOs. The problem with this strategy is that the withdrawal of aid would most hurt those marginalized groups of people that we are particularly anxious to help. Nevertheless, there is some direct governmental assistance and it could be the instrument by which a certain economic pressure is exerted on the Pakistan government. Trade considerations respecting Pakistan are clearly not as central in the weighing of obligations between national self-interest and fidelity to universal moral principles as they are, for example, with China.

Meanwhile, when I spoke with Canada's ambassador to Pakistan, she seemed quite acquiescent to the plight of the Ahmadis. I had a more useful exchange with the counselor and second secretary, who came from the Canadian High Commission in Islamabad to visit us in Rabwah. The Canadian diplomats arrived a little bit before 10:30 announcing that they had about half an hour; in fact they stayed for two hours.

I explained that the basic issue from our point of view is the question of human rights, particularly the right to authenticity and self-definition. This assumes that as long as one's actions and profession do not infringe on the liberty of others to do likewise, one has the right to declare whom one feels oneself authentically to be and to propagandize for the world view and values that one has internalized. The opponents of the Ahmadis clearly have the right to characterize them as bad Muslims or even as non-Muslims. What they do not have is the right to deny the Ahmadis their freedom to testify to their own identity.

My own reading of the Ahmadi situation is that it is probably worse than it was during our 1987 visit and is deteriorating. The fact that the government could sponsor the publication (as recently as 1994) of the hysterical diatribe of the British-Zionist connection of the Ahmadis (see Appendix 3) indicates that there is no willingness on the part of the government to let up on the anti-Ahmadi campaign, which it clearly still finds politically advantageous. The large-scale violence that is occurring in Baluchistan and Sind could well spread into the Punjab where we were located. We were told that the Kalashnikov culture fomented by the massive spillover of arms from the Afghanistan war with Russia has now escalated to heavy machine guns and Stinger missiles permanently mounted on the back of trucks. The central authority does not prevail in large areas of the interior and the rule of law and civil sanctions have given way to gangs of armed brigands who have become a law unto themselves. We fear that if the economic and political situation were to deteriorate further, the government might well turn to scapegoating the Ahmadis as a way of deflecting criticism and agitation about the collapsing economy and disintegrating social fabric, even though the helpless Ahmadis are one of the most law-abiding, circumspect, hard-working, and morally upright communities we have ever encountered.

Yesterday one of the two deputy amirs of the Lahore *jama'at* expressed the optimistic view that Ahmadiyyat actually thrives in situations of persecution. I replied with the saying of the ancient church that, "the blood of the martyrs is the seed of the church," which he readily concurred was applicable to the Ahmadi case. However, this requires a long-range perspective and does not respond to the everyday fears and needs of the Ahmadis. Even though some Ahmadis continue to prosper, they live in a hazardous milieu of unpredictability.

The advocates of the present repressive legislation against the Ahmadis ought not to be allowed to take refuge behind the principle of cultural integrity and non-intervention in the cultural life of other communities. It has to be insisted that there are limits to cultural eccentricities – limits, to repeat, that are imposed by universal human values, ethical standards that enable cross-cultural judgments to be made. This is an appeal to a kind of natural law that is in principle available to all people in virtue of their common human sensibilities and rationality and is, accordingly, binding on all people.

LEFT: The bicycle culture of Rabwah.
Tehrik-i-jadeed official Lueeq in foreground with his children and friend

RIGHT: Cloth bazaar in Lahore with Shaik
Rahmet Ali on left and Idris Nasrullah
Khan on far right foreground sharing the
hookah or water pipe

Conclusion

We had gone to Pakistan with the primary intention of understanding how Ahmadi Muslims deal with the tension and conflict of the ethos of tradition with that of modernity. I revisited the harassment and persecution suffered by the Ahmadis at the hands of Orthodox or fundamentalist mullahs and their government accomplices. Ahmadiyyat is largely unintelligible except against this backdrop of theological disputation (mainly over the Finality of Prophethood) that in Pakistan has escalated to mob violence and penal sanctions against Ahmadis.

On the basis of my previous contacts with Ahmadiyyat both in Pakistan and Canada (and, intriguingly, in Damascus), I had concluded that the Ahmadis in many important ways exemplified a traditional society. They did not to any significant extent internalize the epistemological, technological, teleological, and political revolution that characterizes secular modernity. They believe in supernatural sources of knowledge in the historical revelations of the Qur'an and Hadith and to the Promised Messiah; they are convinced of the reality of supernatural agency in bringing about desired ends; they hold that the final end of human beings is fixed by a divine judgment that results in everlasting life for weal or woe in a transcendent realm of blessing or punishment.

Although there certainly are democratic dimensions to Ahmadi communal life, the fundamental pattern remains hierarchical and authoritarian, culminating in the office of the khalifa who is the deputy of the Promised Messiah, Mirza Ghulam Ahmad. In short, the Ahmadis may be properly characterized as a traditional society.

But though they are traditionalist in the way I have indicated, and in conflict with many of the attitudes and mores of contemporary society – particularly those pertaining to sexual behaviour and gender definition and roles – the Ahmadis cannot be homologized to the fundamentalists who are in fact their bitter opponents. Though dedicated to supernatural revelation and divine governance of society, the Ahmadis do not share the fundamentalist temper of rejection and belligerence, exclusiveness, and intolerance. Moreover, as I have pointed out throughout this study, they do not abjure the Enlightenment legacy of scientific knowledge. The community has a notable number of doctors, scientists, and technicians. They are not Islamic Talmudists.

Does this mean that I look upon the Ahmadis as having worked out a successful synthesis of the defining features of tradition and modernity? To have so concluded would have been too sanguine.

Many times I suspected that the Ahmadis still live so comfortably, psychologically, within their own devotional, liturgical, familial, and communal world that modernity in the form of an antithetical world-and-value view does not threaten them. They are, so to speak, in the (secular) world but not of it. Another, perhaps less gracious, way of putting the matter is that the Ahmadis, for the most part, have not clearly or fully realized the contradiction and danger posed to their religious consciousness and culture by the powerful global culture of secular modernity. This blind spot may almost certainly be attributed to the need imposed on them by the extreme hostility of their Orthodox opponents to concentrate on the defence of their self-identity as authentic Muslims.

As this traditional community, thanks to emigration from Pakistan, increasingly lives a disapora existence immersed largely in an ethos of secular modernity, the collision of cultures (if one may be forgiven a dramatic indulgence) will lead to new and greater problems initially and, given the demonstrated vitality of the community, eventually to new accommodations and solutions.

Death and Succession of the Khalifa

Hazrat Mirza Tahir Ahmad, Khalifatul Masih IV (Successor of the Promised Messiah) died on 19 April 2003 after twenty-one years in office. It is reported by Canadian Ahmadis that approximately 25,000 devotees were present for the Janaza (funeral) prayers held in Islamabad (the Ahmadi research and publication centre outside London, UK), one thousand of them from Canada alone.

According to Ahmadiyya polity, the community cannot be left without its spiritual head, so there is provision for rapid convening of the Electoral College to vote upon a successor khalifa. The election is by open declaration of one's choice: each elector identifies himself and his provenance and then indicates his choice from among the candidates. The college comprises 210 members, 103 of whom gathered from around the world at Islamabad for the election. Since the Janaza prayers must be conducted by the newly elected khalifa, custom requires the college to meet within three days of a khalifa's death, which in the present case was extended to four days because of the lengthy travel times entailed.

The newly elected Khalifa, Hazrat Mirza Masroor Ahmad, is a fifty-year-old nephew of the deceased leader, the youngest son of one of the sisters of the fourth khalifa. This evinces the high esteem in which the Promised Messiah's family is held, Although the first khalifa was not a member of the family, the other four have been.

ACKNOWLEDGMENTS

This book is in some way a legacy of the inspiration bequeathed by Wilfred Cantwell Smith with whom I first studied *The Munir Report* almost half a century ago, and I wish to bear witness to his role as insightful scholar and supportive teacher and friend.

My wife Peggy has been my constant companion of the road on our many travels, most, I must confess, on the rough side, requiring admirable stamina and commitment. During the research embodied in this book she gained access to women's perspectives that would otherwise have been denied me and I am grateful for this contribution.

Our daughter, Dr Sarah Gualtieri, read the manuscript and shared her critical responses with me, especially in the section on gender, where her grasp of feminist issues and Islam surpasses mine.

It will be evident that for someone who does not know how to type let alone use a computer, no scholarly output would be possible without the collaboration of talented scribes. Accordingly, I wish to express my profound gratitude to Sharon Kremeniuk, who started me on my way by transcribing about half of the cassettes that were sent from Pakistan with travellers (we being disinclined to entrust them to the Pakistani mail for fear their Ahmadi source would create problems). I gratefully acknowledge the indispensable contribution of Joan Sweeney, who transcribed the remaining half of my tapes and then skilfully carried through numerous revisions of barely legible text as I laboured to integrate the disparate episodes into a coherent narrative. Muhammed Ashraf Sial and his wife Rasheda were gracious and helpful in responding to my requests for confirmation of certain points of Ahmadi life. The dismay I experienced when I first surveyed the innumerable corrections that copy editor Claire Gigantes had visited upon my manuscript turned to profound admiration and gratitude as I recognized how my text had been purged of infelicities and repetitions.

Finally, it gives me great pleasure to acknowledge the gracious cooperation and kind hospitality Peggy and I received during our 1995 sojourn in Rabwah and Lahore from the officers and ordinary members of the Ahmadiyya Muslim Community. Even when it was transparent that I am not an Ahmadi nor was meant to be, they strove to assist our understanding of Ahmadiyyat. I deeply regret that Mirza Tahir Ahmad, Khalifatul Masih IV, died before seeing the results of our research. I hope that he would have judged our characterization of Ahmadiyyat as fair and accurate.

Note: Because transliterations of Urdu and Arabic vary among informants, differences in spelling occasionally occur when reporting interviews.
Otherwise I have tried to use the most common renderings.

abri	Head and face covering, usually black.
amir	Head of a local jama'at or district.
anjuman	Ahmadi central administrative office.
Majlis Ansarullah	Ahmadi men's oganization.
assalam- o-alaikum	Customary greeting: "Peace be with you." The reply is Walaikum assalam, "Peace also with you."
azhan	Call to the five daily obligatory prayers.
bai'at	Vow of allegiance that creates the covenant between an Ahmadi believer and the khalifa.

bhajan	Hindu devotional songs.
bismillah	The blessing with which the suras of the Qur'an begin: "In the name of God, the Compassionate, the Merciful." Used at the beginning of undertakings like lectures and speeches, and on greeting cards and wedding invitations.
burqa	Garment for observing purdah, ranging from the floor-length "raincoat" to the Afghan shuttlecock total covering.
chador	Women's covering of different styles, typically a large oblong over the head, gathered under the chin and falling down the body.
chanda	Donations to the jama'at by devotees of one percent of gross monthly income.
chowkidar	Watchman, typically throughout the night.
dacoits	Bandits.
dars	Islamic instruction, often following formal prayer.
dupatta	Women's headscarf.
Eid-al-Fitr	Festival marking the end of Ramadan.
fajr	Early-morning prayer.
fiqh	Islamic jurisprudence.
fitna	The social chaos that Muslims believe would follow on the failure to restrain female sexuality through purdah.

Hadith	Traditions that relate the customary practice (Sunna) of the Prophet Muhammad.
hajj	Obligatory pilgrimage to Mecca, birthplace of Muhammad. One of the Five Pillars of Islam.
Hazoor	The affectionate honorific term the Ahmadis use for the khalifa; also a common term of respect in Pakistan.
hijab	A covering for the hair and forehead. By extension the institution of separation of the sexes.
hijra	Muhammad's departure (sometimes called flight or emigration) from Mecca to Medina in AD 622.
ibadat	Religious duties owed to God.
iftar	During Ramadan, partaking of food after sunset to break the fast.
imam	Leader of corporate prayer.
itikawf	A retreat undergone by both men and women during the last ten days of Ramadan.
jalsa	The annual meeting of Ahmadis. Forbidden in Rabwah, Jalsas still take place in Toronto, at Islamabad just outside of London, England, Qadian in the Indian Punjab, and elsewhere.
jama'at	The congregation or community of Ahmadis.
jizya	A poll tax levied on Christians and Jews or other non-Muslims living in Islamic societies.

jumma	Refers to the Friday noon prayer and the mosque where it takes place.
ka'ba	A cube-shaped building in the centre of the Great Mosque at Mecca that contains the sacred stone Muslims must face when praying.
kafir	Unbeliever.
kalimah	The formula of words containing the profession of faith that there is no God but God and that Muhammad is his Prophet or messenger.
Khalifa	The successor and deputy of the Founder, who, in the Ahmadi case, was Mirza Ghulam Ahmad of Qadian.
khatm-al-nabuwwat	The Finality of Prophethood, represented by Muhammad. Orthodox Muslims assert this key doctrine was repudiated by Mirza Ghulam Ahmad, Founder of the Ahmadis, who claimed to receive prophetic revelations. Ahmadis take pains to point out that legislative prophecy is final in Muhammad. The Ahmadi founder is a prophet without a book and without a law.
Majlis Khuddam-ul-Amadiyya	Male youth organization.
khutba	Sermon at the Friday noon prayer.
Lejna	Ahmadi women's organization.
madrasa	Islamic school

Mahdi	Eschatological figure; the rightly guided one who restores the true Islam before the end of the world. The Founder of Ahmadiyyat embodies both Messianic and Mahdist expectations.
Mecca (Makkah)	The Saudi Arabian city where Muhammad was born in AD 570. Focal point for obligatory prayer.
maulwi	Used interchangeably with mullah; religious teacher.
mihrab	Niche at front of mosque that indicates the direction of prayer (qibla) towards Mecca.
minbar	Pulpit
moosis	Those who pledge one-tenth of their income and legacy to the jama'at. The customary pledge is one-sixteenth of one's income.
mujadid	Renewer, reformer of Islam.
mujtahid	Interpreter of the law. From the same root as *ijtihad*, independent interpretation.
murabhi	Missionary of the Ahmadi community.
nika	A legal-social contract, or covenant, between the families of a betrothed couple.
pir	A holy man, typically associated with folk practices and the frequenting of shrines.
purdah	Segregation of the sexes. Also, by extension, the concealing clothes and head covering by which separation of men and women is symbolized and actualized.

qaza	Ahmadi judicial board designed to adjudicate disputes among Ahmadis.
qibla	The direction of Mecca towards which those who are praying should face.
qiyas	Reasoning by analogy, regarded by some legal schools as a source of shari'a in addition to Qur'an, Hadith, and *ijma*, or consensus of the community.
rak'a	Prescribed set of bodily postures during ritual prayer, e.g., bending, kneeling, prostration.
Ramadan	The lunar month of fasting. One of the prescribed Pillars of Islam.
salat	Ritual prayer, usually the five compulsory daily prayers.
sari	Food taken very early during Ramadan, before the day's fasting begins.
shalwar kameez	Characteristic Punjabi dress of baggy trousers and long shirt.
shari'a	God's holy law for personal and collective conduct, revealed pre-eminently in the Qur'an and Hadith.
shura	Consultative body.
Sunni	Largest group within Islam originating in legitimist controversy with Shias as to who was the true khalifa, or deputy, after Muhammad's death.
sunna	Customary precedents set by Muhammad as recorded in Hadith.

sura	Chapter or verse of the Qur'an.
tabligh	Preaching; a practice forbidden to the Ahmadis in Pakistan and other Islamic communities.
tahajud	A long prayer performed in the middle of the night.
umma	The people or community of Islam.
wallima	A communal dinner celebrating the consummation of a marriage.
wasiyyat	Pledge; custom of pledging.
zakat	The giving of alms.

Mirza Ghulam Ahmad 1835–1908, Founder of Ahmadiyyat

The career and teaching of the founder of the Ahmadi movement in Islam may be understood by seeing it against the backdrop of late nineteenth century India. Hinduism and Islam were in varying states of disarray and impotence occasioned externally by British imperial dominance and the challenge of Christian missionaries with their claims of superiority and exclusivity, and inwardly by religious decay and loss of confidence.

In this context, the role of the religious reformer and vindicator was warmly welcomed and deeply admired. Mirza Ghulam Ahmad of Qadian in the Punjab (close to the present India-Pakistan border) first made his mark on contemporary culture as a pious *mujadid* (reformer) and learned *mujtahid* who carried weight by virtue of his cogent interpretations of the divine law. The scholar Wilfred Cantwell Smith locates him within the framework of Sufi devotion and piety.

Mirza Ghulam Ahmad was at first acclaimed by his coreligionists for his ability to champion the cause of Islam in public disputations with the proponents of the Arya Samaj and the Christian missionaries. However, this acclamation turned to derogation as his definition of his divinely appointed status and role underwent expansion. To understand this alteration requires a word of background about Muslim eschatology. Sunni Islam generally contemplates two redemptive eschatological figures. One is the prophet Jesus, the Messiah, who contrary to Christian doctrine did not die on the cross but was supernaturally taken up into heaven, whence he will return to Earth. The other is the Mahdi – the divinely guided one – who will be commissioned by God to vanquish the opponents of Islam and inaugurate righteousness before the end of the world and the day of judgment.

In the course of his study and reflection, it was revealed to Mirza Ghulam Ahmad that he in his own person combined these two offices. He was not literally the returned Messiah, for Jesus, though he did not die on the cross – a belief shared with the Sunnis – had not been raised into heaven, a position that put him at odds with the prevailing orthodoxy. In Ahmadi belief, Jesus had migrated eastward and died a natural death and the Ahmadis reverence his tomb at Srinagar in Kashmir. Consequently when the Ahmadis claim that the Mirza Ghulam Ahmad is the Promised Messiah, they do not mean this in a literal sense but as metaphorical assertion that their founder possessed the qualities and functions of the Messiah ("his power and spirit") whose latter-day return was expected by most Muslims.

Mirza Ghulam Ahmadi's self-testimony was expanded to encompass the futuristic eschatological expectations of all religions for a religious reformer. Thus he became an avatar of the Hindu Krishna and the Maitreya Buddha and even a reappearance of Zoroaster and Confucius.

The *coup de grâce*, however, from the perspective of Sunni orthodoxy, came when he made the claim of prophethood for himself. For the dominant orthodoxy this was blasphemous repudiation of one of the basal doctrines of Islam, namely, that Muhammad represents *Khatme-Nabuwwat* – the Finality of Prophethood. In him all previous divine prophetic revelation receives its appraisal and confirmation. God having delivered his final, perfect, and complete disclosure to humankind of all that needs to be known to guide right conduct, warn against wickedness, and gain assurance of eternal blessedness, the door of revelation is closed. Ahmad's claim to be a prophet was received by the Sunni orthodoxy as blasphemy against God and an affront to Muhammad.

Ahmad had taken pains to safeguard Muhammad's primacy by qualifying his own prophetic status as subordinate prophecy. He was a prophet without a book and without a law. Given that in the Islamic perspective prophetic revelation entails a sacred book (e.g., the Torah, Injil (Gospel), Qur'an), and, moreover, that the essence of revelation is the divine pattern for right conduct, to declare one's status as a non-law-bearing prophet without a book is decidedly to claim a place that is subordinate to Muhammad the bearer of the Qur'an – God's last and perfect revealed book that contains God's final disclosure of his perfect will for humankind. In this way, Ahmadis believe that the finality of Muhammad's prophethood is maintained.

The Ahmadi movement marks its beginning in 1889, the year in which the first converts, acknowledging the founder's declaration of his status as Promised Messiah and Revivifier of Islam, entered into covenant (*bai'at*) with him on the conditions of discipleship and mission enunciated by him.

The Khalifa on Purdah

To convey the Ahmadi position on purdah at the highest level of authority, I quote this lengthy summary of the khalifa's pronouncement on the subject to the women's organization (Lejna). The passage, from Ahmadi Muslims: Historical Outline, *by Nur-ud-din Muneer (Rabwah, Pakistan: A Lajna Publication, 1983), makes crystal clear the importance that the Ahmadis attach to a very strict definition of purdah in fulfillment of Quranic injunctions to sequester and protect women.*

Enforcement of Purdah

Addressing the annual convention of Ahmadi ladies held at Rabwah on 27 December 1982, Hazrat Khalifatul Masih IV warned them to observe purdah properly otherwise severe action would be taken against them. He told them plainly that the replacement of *burqa* by a *chadar* devoid of its necessary complements could in no wise be equated with Islamic purdah, though it was fast becoming in vogue.

He based his address on verses 31–2 of Sura Nur, a translation of which is set below:

Say to the believing men that they restrain their looks and guard their private parts. That is purer for them. Surely Allah is well aware of what they do. And say to the believing women that they restrain their looks and guard their private parts, and that they display not their beauty or *their embellishment* except that which is apparent thereof, and that they draw their head-coverings over their bosoms, and that they display not their beauty *or their embellishment* save to their husbands, or their sons, or the sons of their husbands, or their brothers, or the sons of their brothers, or the sons of their sisters, or women *who are their companions*, or those that their right hands possess, or such of male attendants as have no desire for women, or young children who have not yet attained knowledge of the hidden parts of women. And that they strike not their feet so that what they hide of their ornaments become known. And turn to Allah all together, O, believers, that you may prosper. (24: 31–32).

Referring to these verses, he said that they contained detailed instructions regarding Islamic purdah and deplored the fact that one of the misfortunes which had presently befallen the Muslim world was its abandonment.

He told the congregation that in many countries Muslim women had forsaken purdah and in some of them it had been declared unlawful and its observers branded as culpable. This was happening in countries which were traditionally known as custodians of Islam, but now not content with disobeying the Quranic injunctions they were misinterpreting its ordinances quite reversely.

Referring to Ahmadi ladies in this perspective, he remarked that they constituted the only hope in this matter and they should declare war against this growing irreligious tendency. But, he observed that some Ahmadi women also were succumbing to this weakness and forsaking purdah. He warned them that if they persisted in their error they would be severely dealt with.

Taking the question whether *chadar* could be relied upon as a means for observing purdah, he said that it could be so used provided it fulfilled the conditions pertaining to purdah. Explaining this point further, he said that if the *chadar* was worn only as a piece of adornment which would slip down to her shoulders when a woman was confronting strangers but would be tightly secured on her head and face when she was in the presence of her kith and kin, then it would be merely a travesty of purdah and nothing else.

But if the *chadar* was drawn down from the head to face and covered it fully on both its left and right sides and the woman stirred out of her home without making any embellishments and was fully observant of feminine modesty and dignity, then the use of *chadar* would be quite in conformity with the demands of Islamic purdah. Such a purdah was already in vogue in villages and was quite in order. Women go out to the farms taking food for their husbands or to wells for bringing water for the household.

Quoting the Promised Messiah as authority, Hazrat Khalifatul Masih said that this sort of purdah was also good for European women to practise. He said that the Western women had involved themselves deeply in the economic affairs of their society and had to go out of their homes for fulfilling their obligations in this respect. He said that if such a woman would observe purdah as described above she would be taken to have complied with the Islamic injunctions about it.

Continuing he said that there was another kind of purdah which was more strict than that already detailed. In it besides abstaining from adornments a woman was required to cover her face more securely.

Quoting the Promised Messiah and his first two successors as authority, Hazrat Khalifatul Masih said that this sort of purdah was to be observed by women belonging to affluent society. These women had no economic worries and nothing to do but to spend money and be happy. If such women must stir out of their homes they must desist from doing any make up and must observe strict sort of purdah. The conditions of society were very corrupt and it was in their own interest and to safeguard them from an attack of lustful looks that such a purdah should be observed.

Comparing *burqa* and *chadar* as means of observing purdah, he said that the former device was more comfortable to wear and better suited to observe the right sort of purdah. If *chadar* was adopted by some women instead of *burqa*, it would have to be seen that no Islamic injunction about purdah was ignored. If they were complied with then there would be no objection to its use.

Elaborating further the utility of *burqa*, he said that it had been in vogue in the family of the Promised Messiah (peace on him) generations after generations. The women-folk of this blessed family had worn it invariably at Qadian and it had never hindered their multifarious activities. They had gone for shooting and hunting, indulged in sports, enjoyed strolling and acquired best possible education and *burqa* had not stood in their way.

Continuing he said that now if any member of this blessed family went out with *chadar* on her instead of *burqa* and the *chadar* dropped on her shoulders, this would never be accepted as Islamic purdah. He stresses that this was a wrong use of *chadar* and constituted a flagrant rejection of Islamic values of life.

He said that this tendency must be vigorously checked up in whichever family it was found germinating, otherwise the coming generations might resort to singing and dancing and go to such lengths in immodest ways of life that it would become very hard to reclaim them.

Deploring the fact that women in some sections of society had depraved themselves to such an extent that they walked about almost naked. He said that a lady converted to Ahmadiyyat from such a society would be deemed to have observed purdah if she wore a *chadar* and did not cover her face. But she must avoid embellishing herself when going out of home and also observe modesty and integrity which were the real adornments of a woman. The fact of her coming from such society which had not the least conception of Islamic purdah must be given due regard.

Elucidating the point further he said that the requirements of purdah would be different in different circumstances. For instance purdah enjoined upon the wives of the Holy Prophet (peace and blessings of God be on them) was quite distinct from the purdah enforced on other women. As their practice constituted an example for the rest of Ummah they were commanded accordingly to keep in their houses and not to stir out except for some compelling need. When coming out they had to cover themselves fully. This was to secure sanctity against sinful looks.

Stressing the need of observing purdah properly he said that the moral conditions of people were deteriorating everywhere. Immodesty was rife.

In these circumstances if the institution of purdah was not maintained properly, young girls would be in grave danger of drifting into evil ways.

He said that some cases had recently occurred in which one or two Ahmadi girls living in the USA, had fallen into bad ways and their parents had been helpless in retrieving them. The parents had then realized the importance of purdah but no good could come of being wise after the event.

Addressing Ahmadi ladies he called upon them to realise their obligations and responsibilities devolving upon them in virtue of their pledge of bai'at. He said that they had all pledged themselves to act according to the teachings of Islam. It were indeed they through whom God Almighty intended to regenerate Islam and revive its values of life.

Concluding his sermon he said that if an Ahmadi lady, did not fulfil her obligations regarding purdah and in no way was to mend herself, then, though it would be very painful for him, he would not hesitate in taking severe actions against her.

Our last words are "All praise belongs to Allah, the Lord of the worlds."

Ahmadis as Crypto-Zionists

In my conversation with Canadian diplomats I attempted to expose the viciousness of some of the Pakistan government's propaganda against the Ahmadis as set out in the book *The Ahmadi Movement: The British-Zionist Connection* by Bashir Ahmad. I shall quote particular phrases in the book's summation that encapsulate the government's negative and hostile position towards the Ahmadis and then register some criticisms and corrections.

The book claims that Ahmadis are used by the conspiratorial British-Jewish connection "to meet the threat of fundamentalism." This is highly misleading because it conveys the impression that the Ahmadis are a modernist movement that is supportive of Western values, particularly values of secular modernity, when in fact the opposite in large measure is true. The Ahmadis are in important ways a highly conservative movement as my lengthy discussions about purdah and their scrupulous attention to the Muslim ritual discipline of prayer show. Moreover, they are highly self-conscious about their Muslim identity. Accordingly, the Ahmadis cannot be dismissed as a modernizing movement used by the West in support of Western values, mainly secular, over against Islamic fundamentalism.

The book further claims that Ahmadis "have got a higher status in the society." This is used to justify resentment and hostility towards the Ahmadis. To our dismay, Canadian High Commissioner Marie-Andrée Beauchemin employed the same argument, telling us that in many ways the Ahmadis have brought their problems upon themselves. It is necessary to point out that the Ahmadis, to the extent that they do objectively have a higher status, have it because of their stress on literacy and education. Their young people have close to one hundred percent literacy and the community stresses the importance of education. The class of Ahmadi amongst whom we have generally (though not always) moved are professionals whose children and grandchildren follow in the same vein. General Nasim, one of Pakistan's outstanding opthalmologists, has a son and a daughter who both follow in his footsteps in the practice of medicine. The son of Mujeeb-ur-Rahman, amir of Rawalpindi, is also a lawyer working with his father in his office. In any case the point has to be made that the Ahmadis' higher status, where it exists within Pakistani society, can in no way be used to legitimate the draconian legislation that the government has enacted that deprives them of their self-affirmation as Muslims. The alleged social privilege and economic superiority could be used to explain popular resentment. It can in no way be used to justify the government's anti-Ahmadi policy and legislation.

This condemnatory book against the Ahmadis also draws attention to the mystery of their funding: How do Ahmadis manage to engage in such large building projects and conduct their massive program of social works such as the medical clinics and camps that are conducted not only in Pakistan but in West Africa and other parts of the world? It is asserted by their critics that the Ahmadis are funded by British imperial and Zionist parties. In fact, the funding is not so mysterious. As we have seen, all Ahmadis are obliged by their *bai'at*, or pledge of allegiance to the khalifa, to give either one-sixteenth or one-tenth of their income to the movement. Many of their programs are possible only because of their emphasis on volunteer labour. General Nasim, for example, closes up his prosperous opthamological practice in Islamabad and does three-week stints in an Ahmadi hospital in Ghana that operates eye clinics for the Ghanaian people irrespective of whether they are Ahmadis or not. In his last visit to Ghana he saw more than 2,000 patients and performed 130 operations, including cataract replacements. All of this is done totally free of charge to the patients and without any cost to the Ahmadi movement as Dr Nasim's time, like that of so many other Ahmadi doctors, is given freely. Much of the hospital equipment is donated by *jama'ats* throughout the world. When some American hospitals or clinics escalate to the newest model of a particular piece of equipment, the other is still highly serviceable and is donated to the Ahmadi work in the Third World. The large store of drugs that are left with doctors by the detail persons (sales representatives) of the pharmaceutical houses, rather than being sold to the patients as is frequently (and illegally) done, is donated to the free medical clinics in the villages out in the Pakistani countryside or in the Third World.

The allegation of a British-Zionist connection that allowed Ahmadis to enjoy "the patronage of alien forces of the West and the covert support extended by the anti-Islamic lobby" is on the surface ludicrous. The late khalifa had been very forceful in expressing his solidarity with the Palestinian movement of self-determination and statehood. Nevertheless, he is accused of being a stooge for Zionist forces.

It is further claimed that Ahmadiyyat is "devoid of any charm or appeal to attract attention of sensible people." This claim flatly contradicts the allegations made throughout the book of the Ahmadi infiltration and domination of high administrative and military positions. One cannot speak out of both sides of one's mouth on this question. One cannot dismiss the movement as a grab-bag of superstitious oddities that would appeal only to the ignorant and malleable and at the same time claim that the Ahmadis, through their high education and professional skills, have been able to penetrate and dominate the civil service and the military.

The main point that I have tried to make throughout to Pakistani officials and to Canadian diplomats, is that even if all the allegations of sedition and subversion by the Ahmadis are true, then the appropriate way of dealing with them is through existing treason and subversion laws and not with the theological laws of 298 and 295 that deprive Ahmadis of the right of self-definition. If the Ahmadis are in fact the stooges and agents of foreign imperial forces, then the existing laws against sedition can be used to hit them as hard as the government wishes. What we have instead is recourse to the bizarre legislation that forces upon them a definition of their religious fidelity that contradicts their own self-understanding.

Further I continue to insist that the liberal principle of respect for and nonintervention in other cultures and other value systems is not without limit. A large part of my energy throughout my life has been devoted to the struggle for cultural integrity and national independence and the self-determination of groups with distinctive cultural legacies, histories, and aspirations. But this is not unconditional. I have insisted, for example, that where religious Zionist claims that the entire land of Palestine is theirs by divine gift contradicts the elementary human right of an indigenous population to the land, then the distinctive religious cultural claim has to be sacrificed to the claims of a universal cross-cultural justice. Similarly, the Pakistani government cannot be let off the hook by recourse to the spuriously liberal claim, reiterated by Ambassador Beauchemin of Canada, that this is an Islamic society and the Muslims of Pakistan must be allowed to resolve their internal conflicts as they wish without any contradiction or intervention by outsiders. Instead we are entitled to say that there are universal norms across all cultural boundaries to which most peoples subscribe. The violent and dehumanizing legislation of 298 and 295 is to be condemned on the grounds that even if it were an authentic Islamic implication (which I dispute in the strongest terms), we would still have to object to it, because it violates our understanding of a natural moral law that transcends all cultural peculiarities and applies to all human beings.

Regardless of what the mullah organizations and government officials might feel about the Islamicness of the Ahmadis, I continue to argue that the external state apparatus has no right to deprive the Ahmadis of the right of self-definition. Although non-Ahmadi Muslims are entitled to deny this claim of Islamic status to Ahmadis and to assert that they are poor Muslims or even no Muslim at all, what is at issue is the insistence of the state that people be obliged not only by their words but by their ritual practice to repudiate their own self-understanding as members of a particular faith tradition. That point I have repeatedly made to everyone we have met including the Canadian diplomatic staff in Islamabad and the government officials with whom we have spoken.

On any phenomenological examination it becomes impossible to view the Ahmadis as anything but Muslim. True, they have their own variation on a theme. However, to witness their fervour in the five daily prescribed prayers, to see their heightened devotions during Ramadan, to witness and hear their palpable devotion to the Prophet Muhammad and their scrupulousness in reading and reciting the Qur'an, and to behold attempts to live a thoroughgoing Islamic life as defined by shari'a, communicated through Qur'an and Hadith, is to be confronted with a living tradition that cannot be perceived as anything but Muslim.

So both on the grounds of articulated testimony of self-understanding and on the grounds of the observer's phenomenological discernment of the form of their religion, it is impossible to conclude anything but the Islamic nature of the Ahmadi tradition and faith.

Reflecting further on the allegations by the orthodox mullahs in collusion with the government of Pakistan that the Ahmadis are subversive British Zionist agents, the one piece of evidence for this preposterous claim is the passage in the second khalifa's book on Ahmadiyyat in which he alluded to a prophecy by the founder, "I will relieve the children of Israel." The second khalifa said that this referred to the restoration of the Jews to Palestine where they would find a homeland and that the prophecy was in the process of being fulfilled in the aftermath of the Balfour Declaration (1917), which the khalifa appeared to endorse. It is, however, still an enormously long jump from the advocacy of a homeland for the Jews in Palestine to an endorsement of present-day imperialist Israeli designs that extend to the settlement and control of Gaza and the West Bank. Someone coming out of a Protestant Christian background like mine can readily empathize with the khalifa's point of view for it was, in every likelihood, the dominant perspective within Protestant Christianity. Until such time as the absolutist and uncompromising intentions of the hardline element within Israel became evident and before the brutal mail fist within the velvet glove of pious biblical rhetoric was exposed during the *intifada*, it was routine for Christian supporters of Israel to affirm that they endorsed a state for Jews in Palestine but in such a way that would not obliterate the human and national rights of the Palestinian people. The khalifa's position seems even more modest in that he referred only to a homeland for the Jews in Palestine and not to a Jewish state. His position in no way resembles that of fundamentalist Protestant Christians, particularly in the United States, who have given unqualified endorsement of the State of Israel in its maximal expression – not because they have any particular love for Jews but because they see the re-establishment of the state of Israel as a fulfillment of millenial biblical prophecy that will hasten the second advent of Jesus Christ.

Putting aside these fundamentalists extremists, it is still likely that the majority of Christians, both Protestant and Catholic, visualize a permanent homeland for the Jews in the form of a state but within legal, moral, and territorial constraints that will allow a modicum of justice and self-determination for the indigenous Palestinian population. In this context the khalifa's prophecy calling for a homeland for Jews in Palestine was not an extreme endorsement of Zionism that would justify any claim that he served as a Zionist agent.

There are, of course, differences between the Ahmadi khalifa's point of view and that of liberal Protestants in that the khalifa is inspired by divine revelation with its immutable requirements, whereas liberal Protestants are able to modify their social positions as changing historical circumstances impose different entailments on the fundamental divine obligation of love and justice. The principle point here is that on such insubstantial evidence is the allegation of Ahmadi participation in a Zionist conspiracy erected.

BIBLIOGRAPHY

Ahmad, Bashir. 1994. *The Ahmadi Movement: The British-Zionist Connection*. Pakstan: N.P.

Ahmad, Mirza Ghulam. 1979. *The Philosophy of the Teachings of Islam*. London: The London Mosque.

Ahmad, Mirza Bashir-ud-din Mahmud. 1980. *Invitation to Ahmadiyyat*. London: Routledge and Kegan Paul.

Ahmad, Mirza Tahir. 1989. *Murder in the Name of Allah*. Cambridge: Lutterworth Press.

– 1992. *Islam's Response to Contemporary Issues*. Tilford, UK: Islam International Publications.

– 1998. *Revelation, Rationality, Knowledge and Truth*. Tilford, Surrey: Islam International Publications

Ahmed, Leila. 1992. *Women and Gender in Islam: Historical Roots of a Modern Debate*. New Haven: Yale University Press.

Balyuzi, H.M. 1976. *Muhammad and the Course of Islam*: Oxford: George Ronald.

Federal Shariat Court. 1993. *Quadianis Are Not Muslims*. Islamabad: Darul Ilm.

Friedmann, Yohannan. 1989. *Prophecy Continuous: Aspects of Ahmadi Religious Thought and Its Medieval Background*. Berkeley: University of California Press.

Gibb, H.A.R. and Kramers, J.H. 1953. *Shorter Encyclopedia of Islam*. Leiden: E.J. Brill.

Gualtieri, Antonio. 1984. "Soteriology and Ethics in Martin Luther." In *Encounter with Luther*, edited by E.J. Furcha. Montreal: McGill Arc Supplement.

– 1989. *Conscience and Coercion: Ahmadi Muslims and Orthodoxy in Pakistan*. Montreal: Guernica.

– 1995. "Identity, Multiculturalism, and Modernity." *Policy Options* (March). Also in *Religiologiques* (Spring, 1996).

Houtsma, M.T. 1953. "Ahmadiya." In *Shorter Encyclopaedia of Islam*. Edited by H.A.R. Gibb and J.H. Kramers. Leiden: E.J. Brill.

Kerr, Malcolm H. 1966. *Islamic Reform: The Political and Legal Theories of Muhammad 'Abduh and Rashid Rida*. Berkeley and Los Angeles: University of California Press.

Khan, Muhammad Zafrulla. 1978. *Ahmadiyyat: The Renaissance of Islam*. London: Tabshir Publications.

– 1967. *Islam and Human Rights*. London: The London Mosque.

Lavan, Spencer. 1974. *The Ahmadiyah Movement: A History and Perspective*. New Delhi: Manohar Book Service.

Malik, Fida Hussain. 1952. *Wives of the Prophet*. Lahore: Shaikh Ghulam Ali and Sons.

Marty, Martin, and Scott Appelby. 1991. *Fundamentalism Observed*. Chicago: University of Chicago Press.

Mernissi, Fatima. 1985. *Beyond the Veil: Male-Female Dynamics in a Modern Muslim Society*. Rev. ed. Bloomington: Indiana University Press.

Munir, Muhammad. 1954. *Report of the Court of Inquiry Constituted under Punjab Act II of 1954 to Enquire into the Punjab Disturbances of 1953*. Lahore: Superintendent, Government Printing, Punjab.

Naipaul, V.S. 1982. *Among the Believers: An Islamic Journey*. UK: Penguin Books.

Nur-ud-Din Muneer. 1983. *Ahmadi Muslims: Historical Outline*. Rabwah: A Lajna Publication.

Parker, Karen. 1987. *Human Rights in Pakistan*. San Francisco: Human Rights Advocates.

Petren, Gustaf, et.al. 1987. *Pakistan: Human Rights after Martial Law*. Geneva: International Commission of Jurists.

The Review of Religions. London: The London Mosque.

Shahab, Rafi Ullah. 1993. *Muslim Women in Political Power*. Lahore: Maqbool Academy.

Smith, Wilfred Cantwell. 1946. *Modern Islam in India: A Social Analysis*. Lahore: Sh. Muhammad Ashraf.

– 1960. "Ahmadiyya." In *Encylopaedia of Islam*. New edition. Leiden: E.J. Brill.

Stowasser, Barbara Freyer. 1997. "The Hijab: How a Curtain Became an Institution and a Cultural Symbol." In Afsaruddin, Asma, and Zahniser, A.H. Mathias, eds. *Humanism, Culture and Language in the Near East*. Indiana: Eisenbrauns.

Weber, Max. 1976. *The Protestant Ethic and the Spirit of Capitalism*. [1904–05] With new introduction by Anthony Giddens. New York: Charles Scribner's Sons.

hostility in medical faculty, 143; psychiatric problems, 59

Rabwah: hospital, 53–9; spiritual centre, xiii
Rahman, Mujeeb-ur, scientific falsification of religious beliefs, 9–10; purdah, 85
Ramadan, 29–32; fasting and non-Muslims, 51
Rizbi, Sayed Kamarn (Human Rights desk), 139
Rushdie, Salman: *The Satanic Verses* and blasphemy laws, 135

schools and colleges: Ahmadi sponsorship, 66; expropriation, 59; language instruction, 62–3; nationalization, 67; religious instruction, 62–3
science: apologetics for revelation, 11–12; revelation, 9–11; scientism, 8; Thomistic synthesis, 8

secularism: definitions, 6; dissolution of sacred and secular, 114; divergent interpretations, 128; modern liberal societies, 120; religious pluralism, 117–18
sex: adultery and social breakdown, 89; disruptive force, 87; male and female sexuality, 89; terror of sex, 91, 94–5
shari'a: ideal and practical application, 114

theocracy, 115; integralist paradigm, 116
Toronto, Ontario, ix, 79

Weber, Max: *The Protestant Ethic and the Spirit of Capitalism*, x; rationalization, economic and social, x
Women's Missionary Society, 61

Zia ul-Haq, 7; Ordinance No. XX, 135, 139; posing as a Muslim, 26